CHRISTIAN Golf PSYCHOLOGY

TIM UNDERWOOD

CROSSTRAINING
PUBLISHING

CHRISTIAN GOLF PSYCHOLOGY

Tim Underwood, Christian Golf Psychology

ISBN 1-887002-48-0

Cross Training Publishing
317 West Second Street
Grand Island, NE 68801
(308) 384-5762

This book is manufactured in the United States of America.

Library of Congress Cataloging in Publication Data in Progress.

Published by Cross Training Publishing,
317 West Second Street
Grand Island, NE 68801
1-800-430-8588

Photo Credit:
Black Diamond Ranch Golf Country Club

Printed in the USA by

MORRIS PUBLISHING

3212 East Highway 30 • Kearney, NE 68847 • 1-800-650-7888

DEDICATION

I dedicate this book to Jesus Christ
for giving me the inspiration to write it, and to all those who
would endeavor to spread the Gospel through golf ministries.

CONTENTS

PREFACE

Since the beginning of golf, men have strived to better understand the psychology of golf. Psychologists, neurologists, club professionals, tour professionals and golfers have all tried and, to some extent, have been successful.

This book, like others, is a book written about mental golf, but from a different perspective. Instead of focusing on things like positive self-talk, understanding the left and right sides of the brain, visualization, biofeedback, Zen and transmeditation, I took a different approach. I focused on our human emotions and how these emotions can be used for the betterment of our golf game.

You see, golf is a game that demands control of our emotions. In no other sport do you experience the full spectrum of emotions that is experienced in one round of golf. The ups and downs are enormous! In an instant, a great golf shot could bring sheer elation, immediately followed by grief and discontent a moment later. Learning to control our emotions then becomes paramount to playing better golf.

Knowing that, I theorized that if we really expect to control our emotions, we first had to have a deeper understanding of them. Once empowered with that understanding, we could then use that knowledge and apply it to something specific. Of course, I chose golf!

With that in mind, I concluded I would need a reference book explaining the origin of our emotions; why these emotions were created and how they are supposed to be used. The reference book I chose is called the Holy Bible and this book is a summation of that study.

Included in this book are some insightful thoughts about how emotions both affect and aid players competing on one of the Professional Tours.

It is our hope that through reading this book you will be inspired to make a deeper commitment to Christ and, therefore, reap some of the many benefits of serving Him.

God Bless and happy reading.

Tim Underwood PGA Professional
Author of *Christian Golf Psychology*

1

MAKING GOD No. 1—NOT YOUR GOLF GAME!

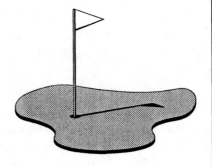

When we are playing golf at any level, the PGA Tour, the Club Professional Championship, the U.S. Amateur, City Championship, or the Club Championship we must first understand that golf is only a game, and should be played like one. A game should be a source of enjoyment, a challenge, a way to unwind, and a way to clear our minds of stress. What golf doesn't need to be is a source of stress, disappointment, depression, or our first priority in life!

THE STORY OF COREY PAVIN

You may not know this, but early in Corey Pavin's career, he had a problem with priorities, mainly in keeping them in order. All that really mattered to him was playing well, and winning golf tournaments. If he played well, he was fun to be around, but not when he played badly.

Eventually, realizing that something was wrong with his priorities, Corey started doing some soul searching, and found his answer in Jesus Christ.

Today, while Corey still takes his golf very seriously, he now realizes the importance of having priorities in order, and that means putting God first in your life, and not your golf game!

Corey's story is not that uncommon on the PGA Tour. As a matter of fact, everyone on the PGA tour has probably struggled with their priorities at one time or another in their career.

Like Corey, many of those players find a way to re-prioritize their life and go on to have productive careers. On the other hand, many of these players never do, and can be found several years later struggling, trying anything and everything to regain their playing rights on the PGA Tour.

Who knows? Maybe one of those struggling players could have been Corey. I mean, let's face it, if all your happiness is determined by just how good or bad your golf game is, how long would it take before the wheels came off?

Fortunately for Corey, he made the wise choice. He accepted Jesus Christ into his life, and made Him No. 1 in his life–not Corey, and not his golf game.

Now I don't know if that helped him win the U.S. Open or some of the other tournaments that he's won lately, but I'm sure of one thing, it didn't hurt!

What about you? Are you making golf your priority? Has golf become a god to you? In Luke Chapter 16, God gives a stern warning about this very thing!

YOU CAN'T HAVE TWO GODS!

Luke 16:13: No servant can serve two masters; for either he will hate the one and love the other, or else he will be loyal to the one and despise the other. You cannot serve God and mammon.

Golf is too important to too many people. Golfers all too often get priorities out of order when they do things like pass up a family wedding or miss a child's important ball game just so they can play one more game of golf.

PRIORITIES WHEN THEY MATTER THE MOST

Have you ever wondered what pros are thinking about when they have to make a slick 12-foot putt to win $90,000? How about the $90,000? The fame? The recognition? Actually, if you want to know the real truth, the pros that are making them aren't thinking about that much at all! There's no better example of this than the story told about Stan Utley.

The Story Of Stan Utley—A Golf Story About Priorities

Dr. David Cook, President of Mental Advantage Inc., a performance enhancement company, tells an incredible story about one of his clients, Stan Utley.

Stan came to Dr. Cook in 1989 seeking some guidance for his mental game. At the time, Stan had been playing on the mini-tour circuit for five years and wanted to take his game to the next level, the PGA Tour.

While working with Dr. Cook, Stan played well in the Kansas Open shooting five under par. Soon after that he won the Missouri Open by shooting an incredible 17 under par total. He was now ready for his next big test, the PGA Tours Chattanooga Classic, from which he received a sponsors exemption. In the first round of the event, Stan stuck to his pre-shot routine that he and Dr. Cook had been working on and he shot an opening round 71. The projected cut was four under, meaning that Stan would have to shoot approximately three under par the next day to make the cut. He did! The next day Stan stuck to his priorities of putting his mind in a position to score and a precise pre-shot routine and made the cut, shooting a 6 under 66! On the third day, Stan stuck to the same routine and had another great round shooting five under par, quickly vaulting him near the top of the leader board. This meant that on Sunday, the last day of the event, Stan would be playing with the leaders! What a surprise! Expecting a real shoot-out that day you can imagine how shocked he was when he saw that some of the leaders had fallen back. By the time he had reached hole No. 17, he realized that a birdie finish would win the tournament! To his fortune, there was only one guy to beat and he was already finished and in the clubhouse patiently awaiting Stan's finish. On the par five hole No. 17, he was faced with a 230-yard second shot over a tree into a green guarded by water right. Stan could either lay up or go for it. After consulting with his caddie, the two of them decided that Stan had been hitting his three wood so well all day that he ought to go for it.

The result of that decision was a towering 230-yard three wood that ended up on the green, just a few paces away from what could have been a disastrous water hazard! After barely missing an eagle by lipping out, Stan tapped in for birdie and was only one birdie shy of winning the Championship. On hole No. 18, Stan hit an outstanding drive right into the middle fairway, leaving himself with a five iron to the pin. The iron shot that he hit from there, in his words, "Never left the Pin!" ending up some 12 feet directly behind the pin. Stan was now facing the putt of his life. A winding, downhill 12-foot putt, that would mean a check for $90,000 and, more importantly, a two-year exemption on the PGA Tour! This putt would mean everything to Stan, because if he won the tournament he would bypass the grueling tour qualifying school, and would finally achieve his dream of playing on the PGA Tour. With all that pressure on the line, Stan stepped up almost undisturbed, stuck to his pre-shot routine and nailed his putt, dead center right into the middle of the cup—incredible!

Afterwards, at the interview they asked him what he was thinking about while trying to make that crucial putt. Stan's reply was telling. He said, "God loves me, my wife loves me, my family loves me, what could be so important about a 12-foot putt?" He also said to Dr. Cook's credit, that he was able to stay in a see it, feel it, trust it routine and put his mind in a position to score throughout the tournament.

This, my friends, is what the essence of golf is all about! It's a game first and foremost, and it shouldn't have any bearing on the way we live our lives. Had Stan truly not had his priorities in order, God first, then family, he probably would have never made that putt, and probably would have missed his golden opportunity to play on the PGA Tour.

DON'T FORGET WHO YOUR PRIORITY IS!

Stan didn't forget who his priority was and neither should you. In today's world things like money, career, the shape of our golf game, etc., often become too important in our life. We lose focus on the most important thing in our lives, serving God first!

God is a jealous God and even though He doesn't mind us playing golf, He wants us to make Him the focal point and not our careers, finances, golf games, etc. Consider what some of the following scriptures have to say about making God first in our lives:

Deuteronomy 5:7 "You shall have no other gods before Me."

Deuteronomy 5:9 "You shall not bow down to them nor serve them. For I, the Lord your God, am a jealous God."

Not only does God want us to serve Him, but He also wants us to seek Him. Consider some of the following benefits of seeking God!

BENEFITS OF SEEKING GOD

Proverbs 8:18 "Riches and honor are with me, enduring riches and righteousness."

Proverbs 8:19 "My fruit is better than gold, yes, than fine gold, and my revenue than choice silver."

Psalm 34:10 "The young lions lack and suffer hunger; but those who seek the Lord will not lack any good thing."

Psalm 34:4 "I sought the Lord, and He heard me, and delivered me from all my fears."

Proverbs 28:5 "Evil men do not understand justice, but those who seek the Lord understand all."

SEEKING THE LORD IS A MATTER OF A DAILY COMMITMENT

In seeking the Lord, you can't just expect to seek Him initially, and then assume that everything will be okay. Absolutely not! As Matthew 9:23 points out, seeking the Lord is a daily commitment!

Matthew 16:24 "If anyone desires to come after Me, let him deny himself, and take up his cross, and follow me."

EVEN IF YOU DON'T SEEK HIM, HE'LL SEEK YOU!

Does an earthly father let his children do what they want or does he discipline his children when they need it? He disciplines them, right? Well, if an earthly father disciplines his children, wouldn't you expect your heavenly father to do the same? You see, God has a way of getting our attention when we decide to not follow Him. It's called chastising, and He'll do it to everyone He loves, including golfers!

GOD CORRECTS WHOM HE LOVES

Since God loves everyone, he will correct everyone. Much like a parent disciplines a child.

In Hebrews 12:6 we read, "For whom the Lord loves he chastens."

Now, let me ask you a hypothetical question: Do you think that God allows havoc to come into some of our games as a way to get our attention? Let me answer that with an emphatic "Yes!"

You see, for eight horribly dreadful years, I struggled with this thing called the putting yips. Nearly every time I was faced with a short putt from within three feet of the hole, I got a nervous twitch.

This twitch caused me to open up my club face at impact and leave all my putts to the right of the hole. It was as if I had no control over it. Every time I faced an important putt, I pushed it right. It was so bad that typically it added anywhere from five to 15 shots a round every time I teed it up! In tournaments, I would actually double hit a putt or two, which got very expensive. A typical 3-foot putt for par would yield me a seven—two shots for hitting the ball twice, a one shot penalty for hitting a ball in motion, and one extra shot to hole the tap in putt.

Now with a putting problem like this, you do one of a few things: See a sports psychologist, quit, go insane, or write a book. Well, I saw several different sports psychologist, tried to quit but couldn't, almost went insane, and wrote this book!

I BROKE MY HAND AND WROTE THIS BOOK

Remember how I said God has a way of getting your attention? With me, it took a broken hand for God to get my attention.

Have you ever tried to play golf with a broken hand? Let me tell you, it doesn't work too well. In late 1994, I was struggling with some questions about my career, golf game, and my purpose in life. Then all of a sudden the worst thing that could happen to a golfer happened, I fell off a ladder and broke my hand. This left me with two months of dead time with little or nothing to do. Feeling a little down one day, I swung by my pastor's office to talk to him about my unfortunate turn of events. He assured me how God had a plan for my life, and through that conversation, I decided to write this book. This book has not only given me a deep sense of purpose in life, but it has also sent me on the way to recovery from the dreaded putting yips! How I got rid of them will be mentioned occasionally as the book progresses. One of the first keys was a new-found sense of putting God first in my life and not my golf game!

PUTTING YIP KEY NO. 1—PUT GOD FIRST IN YOUR LIFE!

You see, as a dedicated golfer, this yip problem that I was having was consuming all of my being. Getting rid of them literally became one of the most important parts of my life! That was until God got hold of me and allowed a broken hand to teach me a lesson.

The lesson: "You are not to put anything in front of me and that includes your problems with the putting yips!" Once I had that full realization, I was well on my way to a full recovery.

While making the journey though, I discovered a couple of new ways to focus on God and not on my yips! To do it, I make a conscious effort in between shots by either reading memory verses, and/or meditating on scripture.

Note: When meditating on scripture, it is a lot easier if you can memorize several verses, such as proverbs.

USE MEMORY VERSES IN-BETWEEN SHOTS

In the index of this book, there are several memory verses. Either use these, or make your own. When you feel a pressing need to focus, pull out your memory verses and verbalize them to yourself. It will help you focus on what's important, not what's unimportant like your score, out of bounds, your yips, etc.

WRITE YOUR OWN VERSES

Since God deals with us all individually, make up your own verses, not only will it help you focus, but it will also help you draw nearer to God.

Should you decide to follow this advice, you will notice the following things:

- Golf will once again become a game, it will be fun!

- You will sense more peace and joy when you play golf.

- You will find a deeper purpose to playing the game of golf!

- You will be more focused!

- You will play better more often.

- You will be playing golf from the proper perspective, serving God, not yourself or others.

- You won't have as much pressure put on your game!

- You will establish a deeper relationship with God!

- You will be able to control your emotions!

That last benefit, controlling our emotions, is what makes up the core of this book. Before we get into that subject though, let's first take a look at our emotions, namely, where do they come from?

2

EMOTIONS AND WHERE THEY COME FROM

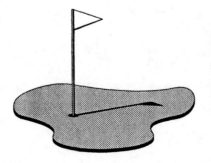

In one round of golf, you can experience every emotion that you experience in life. Emotions like joy, peace, anger, frustration, sadness, or depression can all be triggered by the pleasant or unpleasant experiences that we encounter on the golf course.

In responding to these situations, we have a decision to make. We can either decide to control, or not control our emotions. There's a problem though! When we want to control our emotions, we can't! Why is that? To answer that question, let's consider what Romans 7 has to say about getting into the flesh.

Romans 7:14 - 7:25 says:

7:14 "For we know that the law is spiritual, but I am carnal, sold under sin."

7:15 "For what I am doing, I do not understand. For what I will to do, that I do not practice; but what I hate, that I do."

7:16 "If, then, I do what I will not to do, I agree with the law that it is good."

7:17 "But now, it is no longer I who do it, but sin that dwells in me."

7:18 "For I know that in me (that is in my flesh), nothing good dwells; for to will is present with me, but how to perform what is good I do not find."

7:19 "For the good that I will to do, I do not do; but the evil I will not to do, that I practice."

7:20 "Now if I do what I will not to do, it is no longer I who do it, but sin that dwells in me."

7:21 "I find then a law, that evil is present with me, the one who wills to do good."

7:22 "For I delight in the law of God according to the inward man."

7:23 "But I see another law in my members, warring against the law of my mind, and bringing me into captivity to the law of sin which is in my members."

7:24 "O wretched man that I am! Who will deliver me from this body of death?"

7:25 "I thank God–through Jesus Christ our Lord! So then, with the mind I myself serve the law of God, but with the flesh the law of sin."

The key then to staying out of the flesh is to let Jesus Christ control our minds. To do that there are three things that you need to do:

1. *Accept Jesus Christ as your Lord and Savior (John 3:16).*

2. *Read the Word of God daily, Man shall not live by bread alone (Matthew 4:4).*

3. *Put God's Word into action and take it off of the sidelines (Matthew 13:23).*

Now, if you have been doing that all along–great, you are well on your way! Christ will continue to bless your life in more ways than you could imagine! On the other hand, if you haven't accepted Jesus Christ into your heart and soul, and made Him the Lord of your life, then in reality, you are limiting just how effective Jesus Christ can be in your life. Besides, everything pales in comparison to having Jesus Christ in your life!

THE STORY OF BERNHARD LANGER
(AS TOLD IN THE LINKS LETTER)

In 1985 Bernhard Langer won the event that every professional golfer dreams of, The Masters! Initially Bernhard was elated. He was on top of the world, but soon after that elation seemed to lose it's luster and he felt empty. There was a void in his life that even winning the Masters couldn't fill.

After much soul searching, Bernhard finally filled that void when he accepted Jesus Christ into his life, and made him Lord and Savior.

Since that decision, Bernhard has gone on to have a very successful career, with several wins on both the U.S. and European Tours, including another win at the Masters in 1993.

Today Bernhard openly confesses his faith in God. He no longer feels the emptiness in his life that he once felt, and is now able to enjoy life more to its fullest.

What about you, are you ready to make that same life-changing commitment that Bernhard Langer did? If you are, let me explain how you can do it.

HOW TO ACCEPT JESUS CHRIST INTO YOUR LIFE!

To accept Jesus Christ into your life, all you have to do is ask Him in. Simply ask Him to forgive your sins, believe in Him, and ask Him to be the Lord of your life.

Ask For Forgiveness (God will forgive all your sins if you just ask Him).

Psalm 103:12 "As far as the east is from the west, so far has he removed our transgressions from us."

Believe In Him, Have Faith In Him (To accept Christ into your life you need to have faith in Him, faith that he died for you, was buried for you, and was resurrected for you, that you might have life in Him, eternally, and on this earth!).

John 3:16 "For God so loved the world that He gave His only begotten Son, that whoever believes in Him should not perish but have everlasting life."

Confess Your Faith In Him (Tell someone about your decision to make Jesus the Lord of your life!).

Romans 10:9 "That if you confess with your mouth the Lord Jesus and believe in your heart that God has raised Him from the dead, you will be saved."

10:10 "For with the heart one believes unto righteousness, and with the mouth confession is made to salvation."

Now if you just made that commitment congratulations! You have just inherited eternal salvation in heaven and you are now a new person in Christ; you are born again!

2 Corinthians 6:17 "Therefore, if anyone is in Christ, he is a new creation; old things have passed away; behold, all things have become new."

Now, for some more good news. As 2 Corinthians 6:17 says, as a new believer all things are new, no longer do you have to be kept captive by your old ways of thinking, you are now a new thinker.

AS A NEW THINKER, YOU CAN HAVE A BETTER UNDERSTANDING OF OUR GOD GIVEN EMOTIONS!

In Galatians 5:22, it lists all the emotions that God freely gave to us for our benefit.

Galatians 5:22 "The fruit of the spirit is love, joy, peace, longsuffering, kindness, goodness, faithfulness, gentleness, and self-control. Against such there is no law."

Imagine playing a round of golf in all of these spirits. It's in this presence of mind that golf can be played in its truest form. As a matter of fact, all golfers have experienced this feeling at one time or another. It's the feeling you get when you really love the game, enjoy every minute of it, have a certain peace about it, are willing to suffer through an occasional bad shot or two, everyone is your friend, there's a certain camaraderie in your group where everyone's being kind and friendly. You are playing well and have faith in your ability to pull off difficult shots, you are not easily angered and you are in complete control of your emotions.

Okay, maybe you haven't quite felt that way for an entire 18 holes, but haven't you experienced that feeling for at least one shot? Sure you have, but wouldn't it be great if you could experience that scenario more often?

That's what tapping into the fruits of the spirit can do for you! It can put you into a position to experience God's love, joy, peace, long-suffering, kindness, gentleness and self-control on a more regular basis. After all that's why God created our emotions in the first place. So we could enjoy them and experience life to its fullest!

Let me make one thing very clear though! Tapping into the fruit of the spirit will not make the golf ball fly straight, long, or get up into the air any better. All it does is get you mentally prepared to strike a golf shot, that's it! If you want to learn how to hit the golf ball, pick up my other book, *Four Skills to Better Golf* (listed in the index), a book that is devoted entirely to showing players the proper techniques critical to playing good golf!

Have you ever heard the statement: Golf is 90 percent mental. Well, that's what I call, "poppycock!" If that statement were really true, then as an instructor, I would spend 90 percent of my time teaching my students to visualize, or focus on mental concepts. All I would have to say is "focus," and in a matter of seconds, they would be hitting everything like a pro. Sorry to say, but golf just isn't that easy. Instead, I tend to agree with what the PGA teaching manual describes as the 25 percent Rule.

THE 25 PERCENT RULE

The game is   25% Mental
                        25% Technical
                        25% Course Management
                        25% Physical

* Together these four areas affect why and where your golf ball flies where it does!

Mentally, the game could be broken down into two areas: What we think before the shot and what we think during the shot.

WHAT ARE YOU THINKING BEFORE THE SHOT?

When playing golf, we have to be very careful about what we think just before we hit the actual shot. Have one misplaced thought and the results could be disastrous.

Example: (Thinking before the shot) - "I can't believe I missed that little 3-foot putt back there!"

The tip here is "Watch what you're thinking before the shot!"

WHAT ARE YOU THINKING DURING THE SHOT?

Another sure way to miss hit a shot is to think about something during the actual shot, or while you are actually swinging the club. In hitting a golf shot, thoughts about technique, water hazards, out of bounds, etc., are often solely responsible for a misplayed shot.

Example: (Thinking during the shot) - "Oh no, I didn't start the club back smoothly!"

The tip here is:

Clear your mind of all thoughts relevant to the swing, the target, or the past or future.

In Chapter Twelve, Different Schools of Thought on Golf Psychology, some tips on how to clear your mind will be discussed in detail, but that won't help hardly at all, if you don't first have the proper technique!

CLEARING YOUR MIND WON'T HELP IF YOU DON'T HAVE THE PROPER TECHNIQUE! IT WILL IF YOU DO!

As mentioned earlier, 25% of the game revolves around technique. If golf were all mental, then as a teaching professional all I would do is put a bunch of sofas out on the driving range, throw in some relaxing music, have them visualize a perfect golf swing and then send them home. Sorry to say, golf just isn't that easy. If it was, we probably wouldn't like it.

Golf in reality, especially to beginners, is very much about technique. If I was to take a player who had a problem with a reverse pivot and then put them in front of a water hazard, it's only mental because they don't have confidence in their technique. Improve the technique and all of a sudden that same player won't even be thinking about the water, but the green.

One of the best ways to improve upon technique is to take a lesson from a qualified PGA Professional. Someone whom you have a great deal of confidence in.

Before I give a lesson to a new student, I will often use analogies to get my students thinking about the importance of taking a lesson.

Typically I will say something like, "If you were going to jump out of a plane, who would you be more comfortable taking lessons from, a certified instructor with hundreds of jumps or a friend who has jumped once?"

I will also say something like, "If you were going to learn to play the piano, how many lessons do you think it would take before you could play a song? At least five, right? Well, golf is probably tougher to play than the piano, so if you realistically expect to improve, you had better plan on taking a minimum of five lessons!"

The point: Too many amateurs are taking lessons from other amateurs, when they should be taking their lessons from someone who knows the game inside and out, a PGA Professional.

Today just about all professional golfers train their bodies to get that little extra advantage on the field. Players like Tiger Woods, Tom Watson, Greg Norman, Larry Nelson and many others can normally be seen doing all kinds of training. Speed training, muscular training, flexibility training, cardiovascular training, etc.

GOLF COURSE MANAGEMENT—ANOTHER CRUCIAL ELEMENT TO PLAYING WELL

Golf Course Management, the third item mentioned in the 25% Rule, simply put, is making the proper choices in a round of golf. Like choosing the proper club to hit over a water hazard, or choosing the proper speed to hit a putt, can at times be the only difference between playing well or poorly in a round of golf. In Chapter Fourteen some of the basic skills relative to golf course management will be discussed. For a more thorough review of this subject, I highly recommend Tom Watson's book called *Golf Course Strategies,* which you will find listed in the index.

PHYSICAL LIMITATIONS, THE LAST ITEM MENTIONED IN THE 25 PERCENT RULE

In a round of golf, there are a lot of things that can go wrong. If you lack strength for instance, you may not be able to get home on some par fives. If you lack endurance, you may tire after nine holes of golf. If you lack flexibility, you may experience some nagging pains, and if you lack neuromuscular coordination, you may have to work harder to learn some of the basic skills relative to golf. All of these items together fall under the umbrella of physical limitations and these factors are often underestimated in evaluating golf performances.

MARK YOUR SCORECARD TO BETTER UNDERSTAND YOUR MISTAKES

To find out where you make the majority of your mistakes mark your scorecard. After each hole, mark "M" for mental mistakes, "T" for technical mistakes, "CM" for course management mistakes, and "P" for physical mistakes. If you are like most golfers, you will notice that the majority of your mistakes are made in two areas: Golf course management or swing technique. Surprisingly, you will find that only a few mistakes will be made in either the mental or physical areas of your game.

Now let's assume that you are making some mistakes in the mental part of the game, namely mistakes relating to mentally getting out of control. We've all experienced it or at least have witnessed others in the act of getting out of control. It's when a golfer's face suddenly turns bright red, the forehead develops all kinds of new wrinkles, the brows sink into the eyesockets, and the club slips accidentally out of the grasp. Soon after they make sure that everyone in their foursome, and, in some cases, everyone on the golf course, knows that they just hit a bad shot! As to somehow imply that we didn't already know! Sound familiar? Well, let's hope that scenario doesn't happen to you too often, but if it does then maybe that's a clear sign that mentally something upstairs is out of order. It may be time to take control of it!

In Ephesians 6:12 it says, "For we do not wrestle against flesh and blood, but against principalities, against powers, against the rulers of the darkness of this age, against spiritual hosts of wickedness in the heavenly places."

You see, Satan would like to do nothing more than to get you to play golf in the flesh versus playing golf in the fruits of the spirit. If you don't believe it, take a moment the next time you play golf and listen to what's coming out of the mouths of fellow golfers. If you listen real closely, you will hear all kinds of elicit voices echoing out of places like the woods, nearby fairways, etc. Are these voices of the flesh, or of the spirit? Would God have you say or do any of the things listed below?

In Galatians 5:19-21 those works of the flesh are listed:

Galatians 5:19-21 "Now the works of the flesh are evident, which are: Adultery, fornication, uncleanness, lewdness, idolatry, sorcery, hatred, contentions, jealousies, outbursts of wrath, selfish ambitions, dissensions, heresies, envy, murders, drunkenness, revelries, and the like."

God would not want you to operate in any of these works, in life or on the golf course!

WHICH SPIRIT WOULD YOU RATHER PLAY IN, THE FLESH OR THE SPIRIT?

Which spirit would you rather play golf in? The fruit of the spirit or the spirit of the flesh? Everyone plays in one of them, but which one would you rather play in? Hopefully you are convinced to play in the fruit of the spirit.

Besides, what possible good for your game could come from things like hatred, jealousies, drunkenness, outburst of wrath and the like? Not much, right? Do you think playing in any of those spirits would add to your stress or decrease it? What happens to your body when you get stressed? Do you get tight or are you loose? Tight, right? Is that good for the golf swing? Of course not!

What about playing in the spirit? Do you think some good could come to your game by using spirits like love, joy, peace, kindness, long-suffering, faith, gentleness and self-control? You bet, and those spirits are exactly what we focus on for the next few chapters.

3

LOVE AND GOLF—
WHAT THEY HAVE
IN COMMON

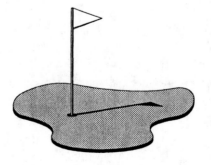

In Genesis 1:31 it says that God created man very good. If that's the case, then our emotions must also have been created very good. With that in mind then why not use these very good emotions when we play golf?

You see, every emotion that God created serves a very unique and useful purpose. Even emotions like anger and sadness. These emotions weren't created to throw golf clubs, sulk over a missed three foot putt, or for temper tantrums. Instead these emotions were created so we could mourn the loss of a loved one, or get angered over unrighteous acts like the murder of an innocent person. Even the emotion of depression has a positive purpose. Doesn't it eventually motivate you to do something, to make some positive changes in your life?

What about the emotion of love or the spirit of love? What good could come from the spirit of love relative to our golf game?

WHAT MOTIVATES GOLFERS TO GREATNESS?

Jack Nicklaus, Arnold Palmer, Tom Watson, Gary Player and Chi Chi Rodriguez all shared something in common. They had a deep and sincere, unadulterated love for the game of golf.

Love is a spirit that motivates, encourages and inspires great players, like these, to achieve great feats. How about Davis Love's win at the PGA in 1997? A rainbow magically appeared on the eighteenth hole, symbolizing the love that Davis had for his father.

It could be said that the love that he and his father shared for each other and the game of golf spurred Davis on to victory.

Have you ever wondered about where desire comes from? I guess it could come from need, like Byron Nelson's streak of 11 PGA Tour wins in 1945. He wanted to buy a Ranch for his family. I guess it could also come from wanting to become respected. It could also come from greed, wanting to have a lot of money, but doesn't real desire come from within. When you have a real passion or love for something.

That's what motivated these great players to play their best, and that's a spirit that you can tap into to play your best. Don't play golf just for the $5 nassau, the fame, the recognition, bragging rights, or anything else, but learn to play it for what these great players do, the love for the game itself!

Do You Really Love Golf?

It's kind of funny to listen to golfers talk about golf. The same golfer that talks passionately about the game at the office can be found just a few hours later telling everyone in his foursome that he doesn't care if he ever picks up another club in his life! Now we know that in most instances these golfers aren't really serious, but it is kind of funny how they contradict themselves like that, isn't it? The point: If you really love the game, then the words "divorce" or "quit" should never be mentioned.

Love Principle No. 1, Don't Get Divorced!

Just like divorce shouldn't be the answer to our marital problems, neither should divorce be the answer to our golfing problems. Golfers all too often just give up because they have a bad round, a bad hole or one bad swing. This just shouldn't be so! Instead, if you have a real love for the game, the words "quit" or "divorce" would never be mentioned!

In 1 Corinthians 13, it says that love suffers long. Now, parallel that to your golf game and ask yourself this question. What about your love for golf, does it suffer long? If you are like most players, probably not! The fact is, if you are like most of us you probably give up on your game way too early, the game you say you love so much!

LOVE PRINCIPLE NO. 2, PLAY THE GAME IN A SPIRIT OF LOVE!

If legendary teacher Harvey Penick was alive today, I think he would have to agree with me, that golf needs to be played in a spirit of love.

There's no better demonstration of his love for the game of golf and his students than what happened right before he died. As a teacher, Harvey was always willing to put someone else's needs in front of his own.

Just before he passed away, he displayed the character trait of love, once again, in giving his prize student Ben Crenshaw one more putting lesson.

He could have and probably should have been more concerned with his health, but that was not what Harvey was all about.

Harvey would not be around to see his student win his second Masters tournament in 1995, for he passed away.

One thing that didn't pass with his death though, was Harvey's spirit. His spirit of Love, love for his fellow man, and love for the game of golf. He literally touched thousands in his lifetime, and that's a heritage that will never pass away!

That's what true love is, putting the needs of others in front of your own. Harvey's life was devoted to that one simple rule, it showed when he gave a lesson and it still shows today in his students, Tom Kite and Ben Crenshaw.

THE GOLDEN RULE OF LOVE:

Matthew 22:37 Jesus said to him, "You shall love the Lord your God with all your heart and with all your soul and with all your mind."

38: "This is the first and greatest commandment and the second is like it;"

39: "You shall love your neighbor as yourself."

WHAT IS LOVE?

Before you can expect to play in a spirit of love, it first becomes important to know what love is. In the dictionary, love is defined as having a great affection for a devotion to or having a feeling of great affection. The Holy Bible gives a more complete description in 1 Corinthians, Chapter 13.

1 Corinthians 13:4 says, "Love suffers long and is kind; love does not envy; love does not parade itself, it is not puffed up."

5. "Does not behave rudely, does not seek its own, is not provoked, thinks no evil;"

6. "Does not rejoice in iniquity, but rejoices in truth;"

7. "Bears all things, believes all things, hopes all things, endures all things."

8. "Love never fails. But whether there are prophesies, they will fail; whether there are tongues they will cease; whether there is knowledge, it will vanish away."

13. "And now abide faith, hope, love, and of these three; the greatest is love."

Now, do you think that playing golf equipped with this full understanding of love could help your game?

If you can answer "yes" to the previous question, then you are starting to understand the purpose of this book, which is to use God's Word and apply it to the game of golf. Even if you were able to play 18 holes using all the characteristics of 1 Corinthians 13, it still doesn't guarantee that you are going to have a good round. Remember the character trait of long-suffering? It might be very well that you may actually have your worst round of golf while operating in the spirit of love. You see, in the game of golf, there are no guarantees!

What would you do if that happened? Give up on the book, render it useless, or realize that just because we have control of our emotions doesn't necessarily mean that we're going to play good golf. Hopefully, you would agree with me that emotional control doesn't necessarily equate to good golf. It just gives us our best opportunity to play good golf.

On the other hand, how do you think you would play if you let your emotions get out of control? If you got frustrated, could it help? What about depressed? Disappointed? Sad? Could any of these emotions left unchecked really help your game?

Probably not, right? Well, if that's the case, then don't you think it makes more sense to focus on the positive emotions that God freely gave to us, rather than dwelling on the negative ones?

A point made for the records! I don't want anyone to think that God is some kind of genie in the sky that watches over my golf game. No, quite the contrary! I just want the readers to understand that God's book, the Holy Bible, goes to great lengths to describe our human emotions and how those emotions are supposed to be used for His glory. I just took His words and applied them to golf! Expressed in a formula, it might look something like this:

BEING IN TUNE WITH GOD DOES NOT NECESSARILY EQUATE TO GOOD GOLF!

I wanted to make that point because I know that as soon as this book hits the press, it's going to be subject to negative reviews and critics. Unfortunately, most of those negative reviews will probably come from conservative religious think tanks. Playing golf in the spirit, or using God's Word, the Holy Bible, as a way to better our game to some may seem like Heresy.

I'll leave that opinion to you. I will say, however, that I'll be surprised if you agree with the critics if you seriously read this book with an open heart and mind. After all, throughout history haven't people come to a saving knowledge of Jesus Christ for different reasons? For some it might have been for financial reasons; others, drug or alcohol addictions; and for others, to fill a void in their lives. So you see, it's not so important what makes someone come to Christ, what's more important is that they actually came to Christ. If a book about golf psychology leads them to make that decision, what's wrong with that?

Now that I have that issue out of the way, let's talk about the spirit of love as described in 1 Corinthians 13. It would be very hard to walk in all of these characteristics on the golf course, wouldn't it? As a matter of fact it may seem almost impossible, doesn't it? That's why we need to enlist God's help to show us how to love. After all, if He created love, then don't you think He would want us to know how to walk in it?

GETTING HELP FROM GOD

God would like nothing more than to teach each of us how to love. As a matter of fact, he considered it so important that He sent His only son, Jesus Christ, into the world to demonstrate His love for us by dying on the cross!

Now, if that's not a demonstration of love, then nothing is! The point is, it's hard to love and a lot of us just aren't good at it, but the good news is that God can be called upon to show us how to love. I think that was one of the points that Jesus was trying to make when he said:

Matthew 7:10 "Or if he asks for a fish, will he give him a serpent?"

11. "If you then, being evil, know how to give good gifts to your children, how much more will your Father who is in heaven give good things to those who ask Him!"

So you see, if love is what you need, all you need to do is get down on your knees and ask Jesus Christ to show you how to love! He welcomes the opportunity!

Another Point! In asking Jesus to show us how to love we are going to have to do something! In other words, we are going to have to read God's Word, practice what it preaches and receive God's instruction. It's only in this type of spirit that God can truly do His work in us.

LOVE NEEDS TO BE PRACTICED!

Can you imagine not practicing your game, what would happen? You probably wouldn't play very well, would you? Well, the same could be said for practicing the spirit of love. If you expect to walk in it, then you have to practice it. Below are all the character traits of love. Try to memorize them, it will be easier to put them into practice:

Character Traits Of Love

Long-Suffering	Righteous
Kind, Meek	Rejoices in truth
Humble	Bears all things

Giving	Believes all things
Real	Hopes all things
Peaceful, Accepting	Endures all things, never fails

How many of these traits do you need to work on? Which one do you portray the most? Which ones are you going to practice on this week? Next week? There's a whole world of golf balls out there just waiting to be hit—people that need to experience your love.

Since love is such a crucial spirit to have, look over this list at least once a month or check your inventory. If you are like most of us, I'm sure your clubs just may need a little cleaning!

USE JESUS AS YOUR EXAMPLE!

It could be said that Jesus uses all these traits. To put up with us He obviously has to use a lot of long-suffering. His kindness, meekness, humbleness, peacefulness, and acceptance are easily seen throughout scripture. He has never failed us, always believes in us, hopes for us, endures and rejoices with us. He's always righteous and the reality of everything He says always comes to pass. Now, how great would your golf game be, if you could walk in just a few of these character traits that Jesus portrays so well? Pretty good, wouldn't it?

LOVE IS THE MOST IMPORTANT GIFT TO HAVE

Out of all the gifts of the spirit, love is the most important one to have. If you truly walk in a spirit of love, then all the other spirits like joy, peace, long-suffering, kindness, goodness, faithfulness, gentleness, and self-control, fall into place. Consider the importance that the following verses place on love:

In 1 Corinthians 13 it says "Though I speak with the tongues of men and of angels, but have not love, I have become sounding brass or a clanging cymbal."

2. "And though I have the gift of prophesy, and understand all mysteries and all knowledge, and though I have all the faith, so that I could remove mountains, but have not love, I am nothing."

3. "And though I bestow all my goods to feed the poor, and though I give my body to be burned, but have not love, it profits me nothing."

Colossians 3:14 "But above all things put on love, which is the bond of perfection."

IT'S THE FINAL HOLE

It's the final hole of your most covetous championship. It could be the Club championship, the U.S. Open, or the family golf tournament, but this is how you feel if you really love the game of golf.

You would feel at ease, have a sense of peace, you are hoping that you play the final hole well, but can bear it if you don't. In any case, you are willing to endure and accept whatever happens. You are particularly aware of your opponents and are willing to do anything to help them play their best. Because of that, the golfing environment in your group is very pleasant and no one feels provoked. Should you win the championship, you will humbly accept it without any sense of parading yourself, or seeking to attain your own glory. Should you lose, you will know that you didn't fail because you gave it all you had. At the end of it all, you will thank the Lord for giving you another opportunity to use your skills to play this great game of golf, which you so dearly love! Right?

By now, hopefully, you not only understand how important love is, but hopefully you will be encouraged to walk in this spirit in your next game. Love though, isn't the only gift available to the believer. How about joy? Do you think the spirit of joy could help your golf game, too?

4

PLAYING GOLF IN THE SPIRIT OF JOY

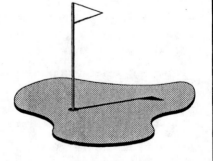

Do you think Fuzzy Zoeller plays golf with a spirit of joy? How about Mark McCumber? What helped Scott Verplank win the Western Open as an amateur? Does Lee Trevino use joy? What about Betsy King, or Nancy Lopez, do they appear also to be using the spirit of joy?

FUZZY ZOELLER

If you have ever followed Fuzzy Zoeller, you can't help but notice how he uses the spirit of joy to play golf. Fuzzy whistles his way around the course better than anyone! I'll never forget watching Fuzzy one year at Bay Hill. It was the last day of the tournament and I was following the players who had fallen back from the field. I saw everything typical of players who were not playing so well. Some players were swearing, others were shaking their head in disgust and I even saw one player throw his club. Then there was Fuzzy. By the time I got to Fuzzy's group, it was clear that Fuzzy wasn't having one of his best days, and I wanted to see how he would react!

Expecting to see another side of Fuzzy's personality, the one when he's not playing so well, I was quite surprised to find just the opposite. What I found was the same old Fuzzy Zoeller that we are all accustomed to watching when he's in contention and playing well. On one hole in particular, I saw him push his drive way right, directly into the woods, his ball ending up in line with a big oak. As

Fuzzy approached his ball he started whistling, just like he always does, took a quick practice swing and then drilled his shot right into the center of the tree. After rebounding off the tree and ending up about 170 yards short of the green, I expected to see him get mad. Instead, to my surprise, he just kept whistling, reacting as if nothing happened. After hitting his approach shot onto the green some 50 feet from the cup, his next shot had an impact on me. He drained the 50-footer to save par! A feat that I don't think he would have ever done, had it not been for his nonchalant attitude towards golf: To enjoy each and every moment!

MARK McCUMBER

Mark McCumber, who admittedly says that he has put too much pressure on himself in the past, said that he had recently picked up the sport of whistling as an aid to help him enjoy his game. In 1994, McCumber was determined, at no cost, to enjoy his golf game no matter what the outcome. As a result, McCumber had his most productive year on tour, capping it off with a win at the World Series of Golf, whistling all the way to the bank!

SCOTT VERPLANK

In 1985, Scott Verplank won the Western Open as an Amateur–a tremendous feat that only two other professional golfers prior to Scott had done. Those players were Gene Litler and Doug Sanders. During the event, the commentators were making comments on how Scott was making a conscious effort to smile after each shot. Scott later admitted that he was making a conscious effort to smile, only in an effort to help him enjoy his game, and to alleviate tension. One final note, he didn't have to make himself smile when he picked up the winner's check!

LEE TREVINO

How about Lee Trevino? Does he use joy when he plays golf? Lee gives clinics on joy! Lee, born a practical joker, is always entertaining. One of the most enlightening stories ever told about Lee is one I heard at his roasting party in Dallas, Texas. It was about the time that he had a big match against Raymond Floyd before he became famous. At the time, Raymond had no idea who Lee Trevino was and was quite surprised when he asked the Mexican caddie who picked up his clubs in the parking lot who this guy named Lee Trevino was. The Mexican caddie responded by saying "That would be me, Sir, can I clean your shoes?" That, in a nutshell, describes the personality of Lee Trevino, and that's why Lee will go down in golf history as one of the greatest personalities to ever play the game of golf.

BETSY KING

After Betsy King hit her second shot on to the eighteenth green at Bethesda Country Club, en route to winning the LPGA Championship, she did something a little out of the ordinary. She started running and high fiving as many people as she could in the gallery. Do you think it's safe to say, that she was playing golf in the spirit of joy?

NANCY LOPEZ

What a class act Nancy Lopez is. You can't hardly watch a golf tournament without seeing her huge, wonderful, genuine, smile. Nancy has probably done as much for the image of the LPGA tour as anyone has, and it's due largely to her ability to spread joy, through the ministry of golf!

JESUS CHRIST KNOWS ABOUT JOY

Jesus Christ knows about joy, He invented it. As a matter of fact, He knows so much about it that He decided He wants each one of us to be filled with it! Consider what John 15:11 has to say about joy!

John 15:11 "These things I have been spoken to you, that My joy may remain in you, and that your joy may be full."

Point! Jesus Christ is not only saying that your joy could be full, but He is also saying that it could remain in you—at all times! Even when you miss a putt, hit it out of bounds, or lose a tournament. His joy is continuous, forever!

HAPPINESS IS BASED ON YOUR HAPPENINGS, GOD'S JOY REMAINS

What happens when you make a birdie? You get happy, right? The "Happening" of making a birdie brings you joy, right? What happens on the next hole though, when you make a 10? Your joy is all of a sudden gone, right?

Not the case if you use God's joy! While the world's joy is only temporary, God's joy is permanent. It's there when you make a birdie, and it's there when you make a 10. Are you starting to see the difference?

ONE OF THE REASONS JESUS CHRIST CAME TO EARTH WAS TO FILL US WITH JOY

In John 17:13 it shows us that Jesus Christ came down to the earth in part to leave us with His joy.

John 17:13 "But now I come to You, and these things I speak in the world, that they may have My joy fulfilled in themselves."

When Jesus was saying this in the 17th chapter of John, He was setting the stage for His ascension to heaven. Before He left though, He made sure that we all had the opportunity to experience His joy in ourselves!

Golfers as a group though, unfortunately, lose their joy all too quickly. Initially, they are very joyous. They are happy they are not working, happy about the fact that today could be their day, and are generally excited about playing the game of golf. Unfortunately, though, that same joy is lost as soon as that same golfer faces some sort of trial. That trial could be out of bounds, putting, driving the ball, short irons, etc., but something gets them down and they quickly become joyless! That just shouldn't be so. Consider what James 1:2 has to say about joy!

James 1:2 "My brethren, count it all joy when you fall into various trials."

Joy then is a state of mind, it a decision to be joyful–joyful when things are good, joyful when they're bad and joyful when things are indifferent.

Let's assume a worst case scenario. You are playing in the Club Championship, the one title that you have always cherished. To prepare for this all-important event, you have spent countless hours practicing your full swing, putting, chipping, bunker play, and you are hitting the ball better than you ever have! You just know that this has to be your day! What happens though? On the first hole, you duck hook your ball out of bounds! Not only is it out of bounds but it flew way over into the parking lot and broke the windshield out of your brand new Cadillac! Did you lose your joy? Probably so! Especially if you are like most people. Did it ruin your round? Again probably so. The question then remains, how do you turn such a negative situation into a positive?

Suggestion one: Look at the situation for what it is, just another trial (challenge), right?

Doesn't James 1:2 say "count it all joy?"

James 1:3 goes on to say that "knowing that the testing of your faith produces patience,

1:4 But let patience have its perfect work, that you may be perfect and complete, lacking nothing."

The windshield was only a trial, the testing of that trial produces patience, and when that patience has its perfect work you will be lacking nothing, and that includes a new windshield.

You can always buy a new windshield and with patience you might even be able to make up for that first golf shot.

Suggestion two: During quiet times, meditate on some of the great Bible stories like David and Goliath, Jonah and the whale, or Noah's Ark. Pull these stories up immediately after a poor shot and focus on the trials and tribulations of some of these great men of faith. It will serve as a way of de-emphasizing what you are going through at the moment, and help you focus on the task at hand, golf!

Suggestion three: Completely disconnect yourself from the situation by turning to prayer. God's got an answer to all your needs and, if it's the broken windshield you are worrying about, it can be replaced, if it's the ball you just hit out of bounds, it can be replaced. Who knows, maybe even your next ball will find the hole, then would you have joy?

Point! God's joy is the same kind of joy you get when you make a hole-in-one. In other words, it is nothing strange or different, it's just the same old joy that everyone is accustomed to at certain times in their life. The difference though is that God wants us to be full of joy at all times, not just when we get a hole-in-one, but also when we break the windshield.

Having joy when you play golf is like adding a free club to your bag. In USGA competitions, fourteen clubs is the maximum that rules allow. Joy, 15th fifteenth club is free. Joy helps you relax, have fun and helps everyone else relax and have fun. Ultimately, that adds up to saving shots. Don't underestimate playing golf with joy, it can really help. Just as Lee Trevino!

Now, if that's the case for joy, then the same could be said for peace. God also wants his children to have peace. Does your game need a little peace? It's the subject of the next chapter!

5

USING THE SPIRIT OF PEACE TO PLAY GOLF

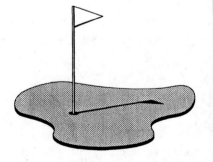

Ah, the peace and tranquility of a golf course! Lush green grass, rolling meadows, rippling water, grand old oaks, flowers in full bloom, fresh air, sunshine, birds chirping, beautiful vistas and the smell of freshly cut grass. Sounds good doesn't it? By design that's what golf is supposed to be. It's supposed to be a game that adds a little peace and joy to our lives. Does it really though?

Unfortunately, for a lot of folks it doesn't! Instead, after a few bad swings, a day at the golf course is as bad as a day at the office. This, my friends, just shouldn't be the case! Instead, you should take the time to smell the roses!

TAKE THE TIME TO SMELL THE ROSES!

One of golf's greatest players to ever play, Sam Snead, whose golf swing can only be described as "peace in motion," is said to have quoted, "Take the time to smell the roses." His point—golf is supposed to be a relaxing sport, it's not supposed to be played with stress, anger, depression, or frustration.

In Philippians 4:8, it gives us a hint on how we can enter into a spirit of peace.

Philippians 4:8 "Finally brethren, whatever things are true, whatever things are noble, whatever things are just, whatever things are pure, whatever things are lovely, whatever things of a good report, if there is any virtue and if there is anything praiseworthy—meditate on these things."

Meditate on this scripture for a second! Whatever things are true in a round of golf? How about noble? Just? Lovely or of a good report? Can you think of anything? Consider some of the following examples:

True - "I truly hit that shot the way I wanted to Jack, right in the middle of the clubface!"

Noble - "I must admit, Jack, that was an admirable shot!"

Just - "Hey Tom, according to the rules my ball moved, that's a two-shot penalty!"

Pure - "These greens are putting pure today!"

Lovely - "What a beautiful hole!"
"Aren't those red birds gorgeous?"
"Take a look at those mountains!"

Good Report - "You know what Larry? My putting is starting to come around lately!"

Got the point? Doesn't just meditating on a great golf shot, a challenging hole, or a beautiful mountain make you feel peaceful inside? That's the key to entering into the spirit of peace, meditating on things that are praiseworthy.

"Peace" is sort of an all encompassing word. Webster defines it as a freedom from war or strife.

DESCRIBING PEACE, FROM INSIDE THE ROPES

Jimmy Gleason, Senior PGA Tour

A good friend of mine, Jimmy Gleason, who plays part-time on the Senior PGA Tour, shared some stories with me concerning some players he's played with on both the Senior and PGA Tours who seem to stand above the rest, as far as demonstrating an ability to play golf in the spirit of peace. Here's what he had to say:

Russ Cochran - "He's from the Bible belt, Paducah, Kentucky. What a nice guy, nothing bothers Russ, terrific mannerisms."

Arnold Palmer - "What a swell guy, a true gentleman, never gets mad."

Gary Koch - "He's another one of those guys, who doesn't let anything bother him, great human being."

Wayne Levi - "Super positive, doesn't know how to get mad, really, really, nice guy."

Dick Mast - "Good Christian man, thinks very well on the golf course, composed."

Larry Nelson - "Very, very nice guy, at peace with himself, gets the most out of his game."

Consider how LPGA Tour star Stephanie Farwig describes the word "peace," as it relates to playing golf:

God's Peace As Described By LPGA Tour Star

Stephanie Farwig

"When I have been in the *zone* on the course, it feels like perfect peace and golf at the moment. There are no thoughts of past or future, just the shot at hand. Being in the zone is the peace of God for me in my profession. When abiding in peace, there's nothing better."

Does peace come naturally to these players? Probably not. Oh, I'm sure it does when they play well, but what about when they play badly? How do they find peace then?

Everyone, at times, needs to find a little peace in this game. It might take meditating on a great looking hole, a mountain, a nice shot, and sometimes maybe they just strike up a conversation with friends, the gallery, whatever it is they do, they find something, anything that helps them have peace!

In other words, they meditate on something true, just, noble, lovely, or of a good report! That's what peace is, and that's how the best players in the world find it!

HOW TO LOSE YOUR PEACE!

In Psalm 34:14 it says "Depart from evil, and do good; seek peace and pursue it."

Just like this Psalm says, if we want to have peace, then we are going to have to seek it, depart from evil and do good.

When playing golf, there are several things that can cause you to lose your peace. Things like losing our patience with a golfing companion, getting involved in coarse joking, gambling, or edging a little bit on the rules, can all rob us of our peace.

GOD KNEW THAT IN THIS WORLD WE WOULD NEED PEACE!

In John 16:33, He says "These things I have spoken to you, that in Me you may have peace. In the world, you will have tribulation; but be of good cheer, I have overcome the world."

In John 14:27 Jesus says, "Peace I leave with you, My peace I give to you; not as the world gives do I give to you. Let not your heart be troubled, neither let it be afraid."

God wants nothing more than for us to have peace. If He didn't then he wouldn't have created the spirit of peace in the first place. Consider what Matthew 11 says:

Matthew 11:28. Jesus says, "Come to me, all you who labor and are heavy laden, and I will give you rest."

29. "Take My yoke upon you and learn from Me for I am gentle and lowly in heart, and you will find rest for your souls."

30. "For My yoke is easy and My burden is light."

HOW TO RECEIVE PEACE

To receive peace, all we need to do is ask Jesus for it. Ephesians 2:18 says "For through Him we both have access by one Spirit to the Father." Now if we have direct access to the Father through Jesus Christ and His Spirit, then all we need to do is ask for peace and we will receive it.

In Ephesians 2:14-15 it shows us God himself is our peace:

2:14 "For He Himself is our peace, who has made both one, and has broken down the middle wall of separation."

2:15 "Having abolished in His flesh the enmity, that is, the law of commandments contained in ordinances, so as to create in Himself one new man from the two, thus making peace."

THE PEACE OF GOD SURPASSES
ALL UNDERSTANDING

This scripture is one of the things that inspired me to write this book. You see, in 1989 I went to PGA School III and learned some principles related to what Carey Mumford, a clinical psychologist, calls the clear key. The clear key is a phrase that is used during the swing serving as a swing trigger to relieve all anxieties or concerns related to the shot at hand.

To use the clear key properly, you simply say a phrase that triggers the swing and lasts throughout the whole motion of the intended swing. (More on the clear key in Chapter 12.) I have been using this phrase, "The Peace of God Surpasses All Understanding," for eight years now and I have to admit, my ball striking and thought process during the actual shot has improved dramatically. If you are curious as to where this scripture comes from, it can be found in Philippians 4:7. Which states, "And the Peace of God, which surpasses all understanding, will guard your hearts and minds through Christ Jesus."

What about you? What scripture would benefit your game? One with the word "peace" in it? How about joy, long-suffering, kindness, goodness, love, faithfulness, gentleness, or self-control?

The Opposite Of Peace, Worry

If there ever was an opposite of peace, it would have to be called worry. While doing research for this book, I stumbled across a book that Dr. Gary Wiren wrote called, *The New Golf Mind*. In the book, Gary tells a funny story about some cards that a member of his carries in his bag. They are called sympathy cards, and this guy gives these cards away freely, whenever he spots someone that needs one. As shown below, the cards read:

Our Deepest Sympathy

We are sorry for your trouble. Never in the long and checkered history of this club has any golfer suffered such a calamitous sequence of ill luck as you have. Our hearts bleed for you and will you please accept this small token of our deepest sympathy.

What about you, do you need one of these cards? Are you guilty of worrying too much when you play golf?

JESUS ONCE SAID DON'T WORRY!

In Matthew 6:27 Jesus makes a very strong statement about people that worry. He said, "Which one of you by worrying can add one cubit to his stature?"

Think about that statement for a second! Now how prophetic is that especially to golfers? I mean, after all, what good does worrying over a 3-foot putt do? Or when out of bounds is bordering the fairway? Not much, right? What do you do then when you feel the spirit of worry coming on? I'm going to suggest that you create a spirit of peace!

CREATE A SPIRIT OF PEACE IN YOUR GROUP!

In Matthew 5:9 it says, "blessed are the peacemakers, For they shall be called Sons of God."

James 3:18 says, "Now the fruit of righteousness is sown in peace by those who make peace."

To have peace in your golfing group all you have to do is sow peace! Say a good word, encourage one another, focus on things that are true, noble, lovely, just, pure, and of a good report.

Jesus said blessed are the peacemakers! If you sow peace in your group, then you are a peacemaker. A peacemaker, in essence, is one who is in the business of destroying worry, the opposite of peace. With worry out of the picture, or distractions, jealousies, quarrels, etc., then your group can focus on what's really important, like playing golf to the best of their abilities.

Okay, by now you might be thinking to yourself, "Fine, this sounds great on paper but the fact is as soon as I hit one out of bounds, miss a short putt, or put a terrible swing on a shot, all of a sudden, I can't help but lose my peace. What can I do then?" Well, if you can't sow peace, then . . .

Get plugged into the spirit of long-suffering!

6

LONG-SUFFERING, THE KEY TO BECOMING A CHAMPION

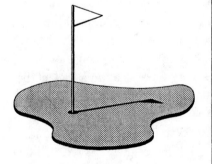

Sometimes in golf the reasons our games suffer are apparent: Lack of practice, physical problems, knowledge, experience, but what about the other times? The times when you've worked real hard at your game and never seem to see any fruit? What do you do then? That's when playing golf with the spirit of long-suffering is needed!

Long-suffering is the ability to gleefully accept the challenges we face in life, learn from them, and apply what we learn to the benefit of the future.

ON THE PGA TOUR, YOU WILL FIND ALL KINDS OF EXAMPLES OF PLAYERS THAT HAVE LONG-SUFFERED!

On the PGA Tour you will find example after example of players "long-suffering" to regain their spot back on the PGA Tour. For some it may be a problem with their swing, others health, putting, or their ability to deal with pressure. Whatever the case, trying to stay in the top 125 on the PGA Tour, can be a real test of long-suffering!

All one has to do is look at the results from the 1997 PGA Tour Qualifying school, and top 125 on the PGA Tour money list, and you will see all kinds of players losing, or battling to keep their rights to play on the PGA Tour.

Some of these players will be seen playing on other tours, the Nike Tour, Asian Tour, Mini Tours, State Opens, etc. It's no fun but you can only imagine how fierce the competition must be with over 370 players making money on the tour each year.

Struggling on the PGA Tour is common to everyone. Below are three different stories about three different professionals who have struggled through some very difficult circumstances.

The Struggles Of Tim Simpson

Take Tim Simpson, for example. From a period of about 1981 to 1990, Tim Simpson was an up and coming star on the PGA Tour. Then in about 1990 he came down with a rare disease called Chronic Fatigue Syndrome, which effects the nervous system.

Now, if you are playing on the PGA Tour, the last thing you need is a disease that makes your hands quiver, especially when it comes time for you to putt.

It didn't take long before the disease ultimately took its toll, and forced Tim off the PGA Tour, and onto the Nike Tour.

To Tim's credit though, he made his way back in 1997 by tying for 37th place in the 1997 PGA Tour Qualifying School. Congrats have to go out to him for his willpower, strength and determination, to "long-suffer" through such an unfortunate disease.

The Struggles Of Paul Azinger
(Paraphrase from FCA Victory Magazine)

In 1993, Paul Azinger had won the PGA Championship, the Memorial Tournament, and the New England Classic. In addition, he finished third or better 10 times that year, the most since Tom Watson in 1980.

In 1993, however, Paul was diagnosed with lymphoma cancer in his right should blade. He called it probably the greatest blessing in his entire life. It gave him a chance to spend time with his family and reflect on his attitude, and where happiness really comes from.

However, it was his strong faith, says Azinger, that enabled him to get through the chemotherapy treatments that left him so sick that he vomited and then had the dry heaves every 20 minutes for nine hours.

"You might not believe this, but I can honestly say, I never said, 'Why me?'," says Azinger. "Two things can happen. You can say, 'Why me, why me, why me, God, why me?' Or you can do an about face and run to God and cling to Him; use Him for your security and your hope."

That is exactly what Paul did, he put his hope and trust in God.

He says, "I now know that when you're 33 you're not bullet-proof. I'm as vulnerable as the next guy. None of us are promised tomorrow. We need to live everyday to the fullest. Quite frankly, I'm grateful for every blessing that I've got."

Today Azinger, has regained all of his strength back and he is playing full time on the PGA Tour. He is showing signs of making a comeback. Recently, he was in a position to win the 1998 Masters Championship.

THE STORY OF TOM WATSON

Everybody seems to remember what a great putter Tom Watson was when he won five British Open Championships, two Masters Championships, and his lone U.S. Open Championship, defeating Jack Nicklaus in the finals.

Unfortunately, everyone has also seemed to take notice of just how bad his putting stroke has been over the last eight years. Sadly enough, the last time he had won was in 1987, the Nabisco Championships of Golf.

Being from Tom Watson's hometown, Kansas City, Missouri, I grew up reading all the local media surrounding Tom, and knew that if there was one thing Tom Watson wasn't, was a quitter, or for that matter, a bad putter. I just knew that eventually he would turn it around.

He did in 1996. Tom won the Memorial and in 1998 he won the Colonial. He was even leading the PGA Tour's putting stats in

February 1998. I guess that goes to show that just because you lose your putting touch, it doesn't mean it's gone for good.

So you see, everyone who plays professional golf struggles to some degree, especially when it comes to putting. The difference though, is some players like Tom Watson and Paul Azinger learn something from their struggles, and come back as good or better than they were before. Consider what some of the scriptures have to say about long-suffering.

In 1 Peter 4:12 it says, "Beloved, do not think it strange concerning the fiery trial which is to try you, as though some strange thing happened to you."

13. "But rejoice to the extent that you partake of Christ sufferings, that when His glory is revealed, you may also be glad with exceeding joy."

In 1 Timothy Paul Uses Christ As An Example Of Long-Suffering:

In 1 Timothy 1:16 it says, "However, for this reason I obtained mercy, that in me first Jesus Christ might show all long-suffering, as a pattern to those who are going to believe on Him for everlasting life."

Compare Some Of The Sufferings Of Jesus To The Suffering That We Experience On The Golf Course

Sufferings of Golf	Sufferings of Christ
Slicing	40 days without food or water
Bad Luck	Nails driven into his hands and feet
Hooking	People cursing and spitting on him
Physical Problems	Spikes driven into his back
Putting Yips	Spears plunged into his side
Mental Problems	A crown of thorns on his head
Topping the Ball	Beatings
Problems with Technique	Slander

Hitting the Ball Fat   Mocking
Course Mgmt. Problems   Imprisonment

Do your problems on the golf course seem a little less significant now?

THE STORY OF JOB

Through reading the story of Job, you can learn a lot about how we should act when we are facing trials in life. Job lost everything: His health, family, friends, and possessions. One thing he didn't lose though was his faith in God. Through his whole ordeal God allowed Satan to have open season on Job, so in the end God could prove to Satan Job's allegiance to him.

In the second scene of Job, Job had some tough questions for God, like "Why must a righteous man suffer? What sins must have brought on my pain? Why are you, God, so inconsistent in your punishment to the wicked?" Throughout it all, Job maintains his innocence but demands to know God's rationale.

In the third scene of Job, a young man named Eliho claims that Job is wrong. He says God cannot act capriciously and punish us for our sins, but claims that God uses suffering not only to teach us lessons, but to strengthen us.

In the final scene of Job, God himself speaks to Job and demands to know what right Job has to question the Creator of the Universe about His ways. Job's humble response demonstrates the depth of his character, and his prosperity is restored.

Job's response in Job 40:4 is, "Behold I am vile; What shall I answer You? I lay my hand over my mouth. Once I have spoken, but I will not answer; Yes twice, but I will proceed no further."

MAYBE WE SHOULD PUT OUR HAND OVER OUR MOUTHS!

Maybe it's time for us to put our hands over our mouths! I mean, after all, if you are duck hooking your driver, what good does it do telling everyone about it? If you tell everyone, then don't you need to prove to them that you can actually do it? You bet you do, and in the end, you will only end up duck hooking your driver more.

THE BRIGHT SIDE OF THE STORY OF JOB

The bright side of Job's whole story is that he eventually was victorious and got back twice as much as he had before.

THE GOLF LESSON OF JOB

The golf lesson here to learn is that in golf you are always going to have problems. Even the best players in the world do. After all, human beings are not machines and are prone to making mistakes! That being the case, the one who learns from his or her mistakes and makes those same mistakes less often, eventually wins. That, in essence, is what championship golf is all about. Learning from our mistakes, and becoming better for it.

7

GOLFING IN THE SPIRITS OF KINDNESS AND GOODNESS

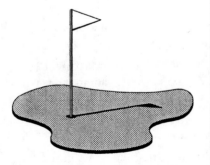

The dictionary says kindness involves doing good to others.

In Ephesians 4:32 it says, "And be kind to one another, tender-hearted, forgiving one another, even as God in Christ also forgave you."

Is that how people act when you show up on the golf course on Saturday morning? Are they tenderhearted, and forgiving?

When you accidentally hit your golf ball into Unliked Charley's group, does he act tender-hearted? Better yet, does he forgive you? Probably not, right? Does that mean you should treat him likewise? How would Jesus respond?

HOW WOULD JESUS PLAY THE GAME?

If Jesus were to tee it up with your group today, how do you think He would play the game? Would He be a gentleman, or would He be without manners? Would He be kind, or would He be mean? Would He be inspirational? Would He be patient, or impatient? Would He show concern for his friends or would He not care? Would He let his light shine, or burn out? Got the point? If Jesus were to play a round of golf with anyone, His light would shine so brightly, that everyone in the group would know without a doubt, that He must be the Son of God!

DO YOU LET YOUR LIGHT SHINE?

As Christians, God has given us a huge responsibility. He wants us to let our light shine so brightly that others not only see it, but they have no choice but to see it!

Consider what the following scriptures have to say about Christians and their responsibility to let their light shine:

In Matthew 5:16 it says, "Let your light so shine before men, that they may see your good works and glorify your Father in heaven."

Matthew 5:13 "You are the salt of the earth; but if the salt loses its flavor, how shall it be seasoned? It is then good for nothing but to be thrown out and trampled underfoot by men."

14. "You are the light of the world. A city that is set on a hill cannot be hidden."

15. "Nor do they light a lamp and put it under a basket, but on a lampstand, and it gives light to all who are in the house."

In Ephesians 2:10 it says, "For we are His workmanship, created in Christ Jesus for good works, which God prepared beforehand that we should walk in them."

Philippians 2:4 "Let each of you look out not only for his own interest but also for the interest of others."

5. "Let this mind be in you which was also in Christ Jesus."

THE GOLF COURSE IS A WITNESS FIELD

I know a lot of preachers that if they were given four hours behind the pulpit to get their point across, they would have everyone in the building converted. What about you? Do you try to do the same on the golf course?

If you think about it, there are all kinds of opportunities to share the gospel on the golf course. There's no rule of etiquette in golf that says you can't talk about religion on the golf course. Don't the guys talk about other things, dirty jokes, the office, sports, etc.? Don't some of the gals talk about things like gossip, shopping, their relationship with others, etc.? So why not turn the tables around and talk about something wholesome like how using peace, or joy has helped you to play better golf, or how changing the priorities in your life has taken pressure off your golf game? These are the things that if talked about, will actually pick up everyone's spirit a notch, and that transcends into good golf!

BEING KIND HAS A WAY OF HELPING EVERYONE PLAY WELL!

If you ever needed a reason to be kind, here's a good one:

To Help Everyone Else Play Well!

I'm sure you've experienced a round or two when all of a sudden everyone in your group seems to be playing way above their head! Why is that? Is it a coincidence or is there an underlying force that seems to lift everyone's game to a new level? While a point could be made for coincidence, I believe that the underlying force is often the spirit of kindness!

Think about it for a second. What happens when everyone starts to play well? Doesn't everyone seem to be getting along unusually well? Isn't there a certain camaraderie among the group that isn't normally present?

That's the spirit of kindness, and it's the best upper that a golfer can ever take!

Ted Schulz Attributes His Win At 1991 Los Angeles Open, In Part, To The Positive Attitude Of Chip Beck!

When professional golfer Ted Schulz was preparing for the 1991 Los Angeles Open he hadn't made a cut in four weeks, so a win probably wasn't in the horizon. That was until he was paired with Chip Beck! Chip, who is known as being one of the most positive players on the PGA Tour, had just recently tied a PGA scoring record at the Las Vegas International by shooting an incredible 59 and was still gleaming with confidence when Ted had a chance to play with him.

Here's what Ted had to say about that pairing: "When I won the 1991 LA Open, I had missed the previous four cuts and playing with Chip did help me because his attitude is always so good. His positive attitude did rub off on me that week and I do think that helped me win. It definitely didn't hurt!"

Think about that statement for a second! How profound is that! To think that your actions, your attitude, and your kindness to others can actually rub off to the point that you can actually be responsible for elevating the level of a fellow competitors' play.

If that's true, then unfortunately, the opposite can also be true! Your sarcasm, your negative attitudes, and your unfriendly attitude towards others can actually rub off enough to negatively impact the people you are playing with. Equally profound isn't it?

Which guy are you? Are you the positive guy or the negative guy–a guy I've named "Unliked Charley"?

WHAT DO YOU DO WHEN "UNLIKED CHARLEY" SHOWS UP!

I'm sure that you've experienced it a time or two. You show up on the course expecting to have a great day, but what happens? Some guy named Unliked Charley joins your group. Everything about him gets on your nerves. He talks too much, he's boastful, he doesn't use proper etiquette, he rattles his change, he bellyaches after every bad shot he hits and he generally just gets on your nerves!

Has that ever happened to you? Did you play well? Probably not, right? Well, if you didn't, it's not Unliked Charley's fault that you played badly it may be yours! Doesn't scripture tell us that we are supposed to love our enemies and forgive one another? To do on to others as you would want them to do to you. Matthew 7:12, "Therefore all things whatsoever ye would that men should do to you, do ye even to them: for this is the law and the profits."

Do Unto Others as You Would Have Them Do To Do YOU!

If Unliked Charley bothers you, forgive him. Just like you would want others to forgive some of your short comings. In Matthew 6:15, Jesus says "But if you do not forgive men their trespasses, neither will your Father forgive your trespasses."

Jesus is even more descriptive when He says in Matthew:

5:43   "You have heard that it was said, 'You shall love your neighbor and hate your enemy.'"

5:44   "But I say to you, love your enemies, bless those who curse you, do good to those who hate you, and pray for those who spitefully use you and persecute you."

5:45   "That you may be sons of your Father in heaven; for He makes His sun rise on the evil and on the good, and sends rain on the just and on the unjust."

5:46   "For if you love those who love you, what reward have you? Do not even the tax collectors do the same?"

In other words, forgive Unliked Charley and look for an opportunity to show Unliked Charley some kindness and, who knows, maybe you will play as good or better than expected and maybe even Unliked Charley will too!

On the other hand, if you are being the Unliked Charley on the golf course, then maybe it's high time that you changed your tune. I mean, after all, do you really want to drag everyone else's game down just because you are having a bad day?

WHAT DO YOU DO IF YOU HAVE A GOLFING DISPUTE?

Have you ever had a recurring golfing dispute in your group? Maybe it's over a rules violation, something like "gimme putts," playing the ball down, or the way some of your friends use their handicaps. Should you just forgive them and forget about it? Absolutely not! That wouldn't be fair, would it? Instead, try doing what scripture says, go right to your brother and settle it.

Matthew 18:15 "Moreover if your brother sins against you, go and tell him his fault between him and you alone. If he hears you, you have gained your brother."

16: "But if he will not hear, take with you one or two more, that by the mouth of two or three witnesses every word may be established."

17: "And if he refuses to hear them, tell it to the church. But if he refuses even to hear the church, let him be to you like a heathen and a tax collector."

TAKE THE KINDNESS CHALLENGE

The next time you play golf, take what I call the Kindness Challenge! Take control of your group, don't let unkind spirits take control. Instead play the part of the encourager, the inspirer, the peacemaker and the Mr. Nice guy.

Instead of allowing everyone else's negative sarcasms to ruin the game, turn the tables around on your golfing buddies. Encourage everyone in the group to play a part in helping each other play their best. Make it a standing rule in your group.

That might mean setting some boundaries like staying focused, talking about wholesome, not negative things in between shots, encouraging one another, etc. This sounds like golf etiquette, doesn't it? Isn't that the way the game is supposed to be played anyway?

ENCOURAGE EACH OTHER TO PLAY GOOD

Yoo many friends play golf encouraging one another to fail when instead they should be encouraging on another to succeed.

Several years ago, I worked as an Assistant Golf Professional at Brookhaven Country Club in Dallas, Texas. As juniors Scott Verplank and Andrew Magee of the PGA Tour, and Brian Watts of the Japan Tour, grew up playing against one another. It's no surprise that all three are having very successful careers.

A funny thing happens when people compete. If one player shoots 68, then the next guy wants to shoot 67. In other words good play feeds off of good play. The lower your buddy shoots, the lower you will shoot, or vice versa.

That's why it's so important to encourage one another in a good spirited rivalry. Encourage each other to make putts, hit greens, and shoot low scores. Creating this type of atmosphere in your group only leads to good play.

I don't know how many times I've seen just the opposite occur. A good spirited rivalry between friends turns ugly. Fights break out and things like priding, jealousies, sarcasm, etc., have a way of disrupting everyones game. The results can be devastating. Don't underestimate their effects. I've even seen best of friends become adversaries.

This just shouldn't be so! That's why it is so important for the Nice Guy to stand up and take control. What about you, are you the Mr. Nice Guy? Are you going to let your light shine?

WHAT IF UNLIKED CHARLEY WON'T CHANGE?

Well, then I guess you are just going to have to put up with him. Consider what Colossians has to say about the subject:

Colossians 3:12 "Therefore as elect of God, holy and beloved, put on tender mercies, kindness, humility of mind, meekness, longsuffering."

3:13 "Bearing with one another, and forgiving one another, if anyone has a complaint against another, even as Christ forgave you, so you must also do."

3:14 "But above all things put on love which is the bond of perfection."

In these verses, Christ is not only telling us to be kind, but to forgive one another for their faults. Let's face it, in life there are going to be a lot of things that distract us. We have a choice to make. We can either let these things get under our skin, or we can accept them. If we can accept them, then we can get back to what's important, and when it's playing golf, it's beating old man par!

PLAYING AGAINST OLD MAN PAR—BOBBY JONES

Have you ever heard this statement before, made by the great Bobby Jones? Bobby learned a long time ago that it wasn't the other players that he was playing against, but he was playing against the golf course and old man par.

Bobby was smart enough that he didn't let outside obstacles bother him. Competitors, bothersome fans, media, etc. The only thing that he focused on was the hole and what he had to do to make par!

What do you focus on when you play–the hole? Your score? Who you are playing with? Old man par? If you are smart, you would do what Bobby Jones did and just try to focus on beating old man par! (For some of you that may be old man bogey, double bogey, or maybe even quadruple bogey, but whatever it is try to do your best, to beat old man par!)

Playing golf in a spirit of kindness then involves three things: Good works, being kind to others, and playing golf against old man par! If you can do that, then the other distractions like Unliked Charley's, score, etc., won't bother you.

Beating old man par isn't as easy as being kind though. It takes a little faith. As a matter of fact, everything that we do through Christ takes a little faith!

8

FAITH, THE KEY TO PLAYING IN ALL THE SPIRITS

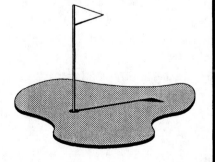

If you were to think about it, faith is what we use to activate all of God's spirits. We have to use faith to love at times when we don't feel like loving. We have to use faith when we try to experience joy in some of our most trying moments. We have to use faith to enter into God's peace. Faith is what we use during times of suffering: Long-suffering. At times we even have to use faith in God when we are trying to be kind to those we really don't care to be kind to. We even have to use faith when we use the spirit of gentleness, like right after we miss a 3-foot putt! Faith knows about fighting! The fight to stay focused, to use love, joy, peace, long-suffering, gentleness, kindness, and self-control.

FAITH KNOWS HOW TO FIGHT!

If you play golf in a spirit of faith, you know how to fight the good fight. The fight against old man par, the fight to stay focused, to not give up, to stay in control and to not let your temper flare. That's what faith is all about. Consider what Timothy says about the fight of faith:

In 2 Timothy 4:7 it says "I have fought the good fight, I have finished the race, I have kept the faith."

When we play golf, more often than not, doesn't it seem like a real struggle? Hit it out of bounds, miss a putt, shank a wedge, get a bad bounce, and all of a sudden golf doesn't seem like a walk in the park anymore, does it?

It's at times like these that you really have to fight the war of faith. If you don't, playing one shot at a time or staying focused is impossible!

PLAYING GOLF ONE SHOT AT A TIME!

Have you actually ever successfully played an entire 18 holes of golf one shot at a time, anyway? You know, the round where you focused just as hard over a 3-foot putt as you did when you were faced with a 250-yard carry over water? Probably not, right? Why is that anyway? Do you think it might have something to do with getting too wrapped up in what we see missed putts, missed shots, etc.? Sure we do, and that's where the spirit of faith can help out, because faith only hopes, confidence only sees!

In 2 Corinthians 5:7 it says, "We walk by faith, not by sight."

FAITH HOPES, CONFIDENCE SEES!

Probably the biggest difference between confidence and faith is that faith hopes, confidence sees. Consider what Hebrews has to say about faith:

Hebrews 11:1 "Now faith is the substance of things hoped for, the evidence of things not seen."

See the difference? Confidence is past tense, putts already made, tournaments already won, where faith is future tense, putts that will eventually be made, scores that will eventually be shot, and tournaments that will eventually be won.

Faith is always positive where confidence can at times be negative.

I'm sure it's happened to you before. You are playing a round of golf, with an unusual amount of confidence, and then all of a sudden miss a short makeable putt. If you can forget it, great, but what if you don't? Don't you start to lose confidence?

Not so with faith. You see, if you are using faith and you miss that same short putt, no problem, it's forgotten isn't it? Isn't faith the substance of things hoped for, the evidence of things not seen? Starting to see my point?

You see, faith is positive because it involves hope in the future. But what do you do if you lack faith?

If You Lack Faith, Take A Lesson From Someone You Have Faith In!

Several times in this book I have eluded to the fact that for eight years I had a dreadful problem with the putting yips. During that whole period, I never had any faith in my technique. That was until I took a putting lesson from Rod.

A friend of mine, Rod Yeager, who is a fellow PGA Professional, finally got my putter working for me one day when he showed me what he calls the "Rock and Roll" method. I had seen Rod use this method several times in practice and in tournaments and was always amazed at how well he putted. Below is a stat sheet that Rod has kept since 1979 of his best rounds. What I find amazing is his stats for putts per round. On one occasion, he actually used only 22 putts, and that was after hitting 12 greens. On two other occasions, he used only 23 putts, while still hitting 12 and 11 greens, respectively.

With those kinds of credentials, I was all open-ears when I finally talked Rod into showing me his technique.

The technique itself is a little unorthodox in that the putter isn't swung on a conventional inside-to-square to inside line, but the putter head is actually swung from closed to square-to-open. It took a little getting used to at first, but once I started getting used to it, I started making putts from everywhere. I actually beat Rod in a little putting duel with his own technique!

Today I actually enjoy putting, and that's all because I have faith! Refer to the chart below for Rod Yeager's putting stats:

PUTTING YIP KEY NO. 2: FIND A GOOD TEACHER THAT YOU HAVE A GREAT DEAL OF FAITH IN!

Rod Yeager's Putting Stats–During best rounds 1979 to Present

number of putts/3 putts and no. of putts per GIR	Score	Greens in Reg. (GIR)
24 (One 3 Putt)	65	13
28	66	16
26 1.57	66	14
29 (one 3 putt) 1.73	64	15
27 1.69	67	13
31 (one 3 putt) 1.68	67	16
29 1.69	67	13
26 1.61	67	13
29 1.64	66	17
27 1.57	66	14
27 1.60	64	15
28 1.60	66	15
25 1.54	67	11
28 (One 3 putt)		
28 1.58	64	17
28 1.66	66	15
22 * 1.33	63	12
25 1.50	64	14
27 1.64	66	14
26 1.58	67	12
23 (One 3 putt)		
23 1.25	65	12
23 (One 3 putt)		
23 1.36	65	11
28 (One 3 putt)		
28 1.64	67	14

* about 1.719 putts per round usually leads the PGA Tour.

PUTTING YIP KEY NO. 3:
USE A LITTLE PATIENCE

Without God's patience I don't think I would have ever kept playing golf. I mean let's face it, when you spend a majority of your life learning how to hit a golf ball, finally do, and then a little thing like short putts keeps you from reaching your potential, it can at times be pretty frustrating, can't it? That's when you need to use the spirit of patience.

FAITH AND PATIENCE

If you were to think about it, faith and patience resemble each other. When Noah built the Ark, he had to have faith that it would rain and patience to wait for it to rain.

When Moses took the Israelites into the desert, he had to have faith that they would eventually reach the Promised Land. It took 40 years of patience to finally get there.

When Elizabeth believed God would give her a son, she had to have faith, and having a child at her age had to take a lot of patience.

See the parallel?

GOD'S PATIENCE-LPGA TOUR STAR STEPHANIE FARWIG

My career has been one of patience. I have competed on the LPGA Tour for 14 years and am still looking for my first win. I finished second six times so I've been right there enough times to know that it will be in the Lord's timing when I do win. The scripture I usually take with me when I'm in contention is 2 Timothy 1:7 "God did not give us a spirit of fear, but of power, love and a sound mind." God never wants us fearful but instead confident with love for others and the game.

THE PATIENCE OF WOODY AUSTIN

A good friend of mine, Dean Atkinson, use to caddie for Woody Austin and shared a few stories about him with me. For one, as has been much publicized, Woody worked as a bank teller while trying to make it on the PGA Tour.

What I found particularly interesting about his story, is that unlike most tour stars, he didn't come from a wealthy family, and had to work extra hard for every dollar he earned.

To prepare himself for competitive golf, he played on the Japan Tour in 1989 and 1990 and on the Mini Tours in 1992 and 1993. In 1993, he took out a $2,000 dollar loan to try to qualify for a Nike event. He qualified and from there he was off and running, playing full time on the Nike Tour in 1994 and playing his first full year on the PGA Tour in 1995.

In speaking about Woody's mannerisms, Dean said that Woody can often be heard saying after he hits a bad shot something like, "Patience, it will come. Patience, it will come."

I guess his patience did come. In 1995 he ranked 24th on the PGA Tour money list, and 1996 he finished 32nd—not too bad for a former bank teller!

PATIENCE IS WHAT'S NEEDED TO WIN A U.S. OPEN?

To win a U.S. Open, there's no way to get around it—you have to use patience! After all, what do you have to use when you think you hit a great shot, only to find your ball buried in rough, three to six inches thick? What do you use when you know that par is as good as a score as you can get, and what do you use to sustain your inner emotions when you are faced with one demanding shot after another. Patience, right? Consider some of the following examples:

EXAMPLES OF PATIENCE AT THE U.S. OPEN

• When Steve Jones beat out fellow Christian friend Tom Lehman in the 1996 Open, he had to do it with a reverse overlapping grip to protect against an injury he had to his left ring finger. It was his first full season he had been able to play since a dirt bike injury in 1991.

• Under intense pressure from the media, the best player to never win a major, Corey Pavin, cast the monkey off his back, by solidly striking a four wood into the last green to win the 1995 U.S. Open at Shinnecock Hills.

• In 1992, Tom Kite cast the same monkey off his back, by beating out Jeff Sluman under tough conditions at Pebble Beach, to win his first Open.

• Hale Irwin had to use a lot of patience in the 1990 Open. Remember the 19-hole playoff at Medinah against Mike Donald?

• How about Scott Simpson in the 1987 Open? He barely escaped the ever-present Tom Watson at the Olympic Club. Scott even commented on his patience during the post-interview wrap-up.

• And, finally, how about Tom Watson's famous chip in on the seventeenth hole at Pebble Beach to defeat Jack Nicklaus in 1982? Now, when you are going up against a man that has four Opens to his credit, you obviously have to use a lot of patience if you ever expect to catch him. He finally did on hole No. 17.

Hopefully, from these examples, you can see just how important it is to have patience when you are playing golf, really on any level, but especially at the U.S. Open.

If you expect to win at the Open, you better not only have patience, but it better be perfect and complete!

LET YOUR PATIENCE BE PERFECT AND COMPLETE

In James 1:4 it says, "But let patience have its perfect work, that you may be perfect and complete, lacking nothing."

Patience—Perfect and complete, lacking nothing!

Meditate on these three words for a second: "Patience," "perfect" and "complete," and apply those words to your golf game. If your patience is perfect and complete, nothing would bother you because you are secure in Christ Jesus. It wouldn't matter what happened: Missed putts, missed cuts, bad scores, out of bounds, no matter what the circumstance, if your patience was perfect and complete, you would lack nothing! Right? That's what the spirit of faith, or patience is all about, and that's what Larry, Scott, Tom, Corey, and a lot of other pros rely on to win the U.S. Open.

FAITH CAN ALSO GET RID OF ANXIETY

If you are approaching golf with a lot of anxiety, worry or fear, then you are almost certain to set yourself up for a letdown.

Golf, more so than other sports, requires a clear and uncluttered mind. In some sports like football, for instance, heightened emotions like fear, anger and frustration can actually at times improve a player's performance, but not in golf.

Golf is a sport that needs to be played on an even emotional keel. Heightened emotions like anger and exuberance can actually do more harm than good for a golfer's game—especially if not kept in check! That's why I like to think of golf as a walk of faith, and not a walk of worry, fear, anxiety or frustration.

DON'T BE SCARED TO WALK ON THE WATER

The story told in Mark 4:40 is one about Peter's lack of faith. Peter, a follower of Christ, knew that Christ could do many great and wonderful works, but when it came time to take a step on the water, Peter feared for his life.

Kind of sounds like a golfer who is scared to death of carrying a 200-yard water hazard, doesn't it? It's no different! What's there to fear anyway? Aren't we just playing a game? What's going to happen if you play badly? Is your wife going to stop loving you? What about your dog, is he going to quit wagging his tail when he sees you? How about Christ, is He going to stop loving you? You see, when it comes to fear, there's really nothing to fear at all, especially if you are secure in Christ Jesus. Consider what Mark 4:40 has to say about the subject:

Mark 4:40 "…Why are you so fearful? How is it that you have no faith?"

WHY GOLFERS HAVE STREAKS

Have you ever wondered why golfers are so streaky? Why is it that we have a good hole, have three or four more good holes, and then all of a sudden go into a slump? Is it because our abilities all of a sudden leave us, or is it our confidence?

In most cases, it's our confidence. Why is that though? Isn't it because we start thinking things like, "When is this hot streak going to end?" or "I don't normally play this good," or "I'm probably going to choke again." Sure we do. Our anxieties or fears about messing up a good game nearly get us every time! How then can we ward off those fears?

USE FAITH, NOT CONFIDENCE, BUT FAITH!

The faith that says "I love this game," the faith that says "I have peace through God, not fear but peace," the faith that says, "I'm going to fight it out–long-suffering," the faith that says, "be gentle, that missed three footer doesn't bother me," the faith that says "I'm going to be kind to that Unliked Charley even if I don't want to," the faith that says "I'm going to enjoy this day no matter what!" Finally the faith that says, "I'm going to use faith–faith in my abilities to play better golf!"

9

PLAYING GOLF IN A SPIRIT OF GENTLENESS

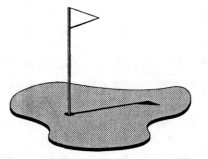

Isn't golf supposed to be a gentleman's game? When golf was invented in the 1500s, etiquette was such a part of the game that it didn't matter who you were playing with, the game was fun for everyone involved. In the 1970s, that heritage was still very rich, in the 1980s golf was still sort of a gentleman's and lady's game, but what about the 1990s? Is golf still a gentleman's and lady's game today? Hard to answer that question, isn't it? I mean, how many gentlemen and ladies do you actually run into on the golf courses of America today? Not as many, right? Well, that just shouldn't be the case, that's why it's so important that as a cooperative band of Christians, we need to introduce gentleman-like qualities back into the game of golf.

REINTRODUCING GENTLEMAN-LIKE QUALITIES BACK INTO THE GAME OF GOLF!

If there was ever a time to reintroduce the gentleman-like qualities back onto the golf courses of America, now is the time! On too many of our courses, foursomes can generally be seen using lewd language, yelling at players that get in their way, disrespecting golf course policies and procedures and, in some cases, actually fighting with other golfers. That's right, fighting! I've actually been the witness of two players coming into the pro shop covered with blood from head to toe, after getting involved in an altercation on the golf course. It was all because an errant tee shot landed nearby, it didn't even hit anyone! Pretty sad, isn't it? To think that actions like these are starting to become all too much commonplace. How can people be so mean, nasty, rude, impatient and distasteful when they should be having fun. Where are the gentlemen?

WHERE ARE THE GENTLEMEN AND LADIES?

What is a gentleman anyway? Well, if you were to look it up in the dictionary, it would be described as a man of high honor, a comprehending nobleman, a man of good social position.

JESUS WAS A GENTLEMAN

Jesus was a gentleman. Did you ever hear of Him complaining when He was thrown into prison? Was He impatient or patient with people? Was He courteous? Did He come to serve or be served? Did He have a social grace about Him? The answer, of course, to all of these questions is "yes," He was all these things and more. Jesus was in the true sense of the word, a gentleman!

In Matthew 11:29 we learn some insight into the gentleness of Jesus when he says, "Take my yoke upon you and learn from Me, for I am gentle and lowly in heart, and you will find rest for your souls."

EVER HEARD OF GENTLE BEN CRENSHAW, THE GENTLEMAN

As a two-time Master Champion, Gentle Ben as he is called because he is such a gentleman, uses the character trait of gentleness as good as anyone, every time he crafts his way around the layout at Augusta National. His record there is phenomenal! Winning twice, once in 1995 and also in 1984, not to mention all his finishes in the top 10.

Without gentleness, you simply can't win at Augusta. Hit a 3-foot putt one foot too far at Augusta, and you just may find yourself

80 feet away. Hit an approach shot to the wrong part of the green and making par is out of the question. Get too aggressive on the wrong hole and double and triple bogeys are not out of the ordinary. Augusta National has been made famous, because it is a golf course that demands gentleness and Ben Crenshaw has been made famous, because he is the King of Gentleness!

Ben, though, isn't the only one who exudes this spirit of gentleness at the Masters. What about Jack Nicklaus in winning the Masters six times, or Nick Faldo in winning it three times, or Bernhard Langer in winning it twice.?

In watching the Masters, you never know what to expect. It seems that every year you just sit on the edge of your chair, waiting for some great drama to unfold. Like Tom Watson's famous one-shot win over Jack Nicklaus in 1977, or Jack Nicklaus's sixth Masters title in 1986 at the ripe old age of 46, or Larry Mize's gentle 170-foot chip in on the first extra play-off hole to beat out Greg Norman in 1987, and, of course, Ben Crenshaw's famous win in 1995, in paying tribute to the death of his life-long teacher, Harvey Penick.

Augusta is about gentleness. It's about man meeting nature, it's about heritage, friends of old, traditions, mannerisms and mystique. The whole experience and ambiance of the Masters seems to absorb everyone from the players to the galleries, and to those of us watching at home.

What does it take to win at the Masters? A great short game? Yes. Long accurate woods? Again, yes. But do you want to know what the real secret is? If you ask me, I think it can be found in the spirit of gentleness. Name anyone who has won at the Masters, and you will find they were all gentlemen!

10

CONTROL OF YOURSELF— SELF-CONTROL

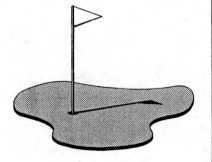

Self-control by definition means control of yourself. By choosing to read this book you are exercising self-control. On the golf course you exercise self-control when you choose not to get angry after hitting a bad shot. What then would you call it when you get angry?

The Opposite Of Self-Control—Out Of Control

If there was an opposite of self-control, it would have to be called out of control. On the golf course you reach this stage when you simply can no longer tolerate yourself, your game, or for that matter the game of golf.

Now let's hope you don't reach this tolerance level often, but if you do then maybe that's a clear cut sign that you are losing the war against your flesh!

Self-Control Versus The War Of The Flesh!

Self-control could also be viewed as control over the flesh. Everyone struggles with something. For some, it is a struggle with diets, alcohol, drugs, sex, pornography, exercise, tobacco, watching TV, or procrastinating, but everyone has some degree of problem with self-control. Most of these problems can be traced back to one thing though, listening to lies!

In a book entitled *Finding the Freedom of Self-Control,* author William Backus conquers the problem of self-control. The problem, lies! We struggle with self-control because we listen to lies, instead of the truth!

In John 8:32 it says "And you shall know the truth, and the truth shall make you free."

Now, if we know the truth, then doesn't it make sense that we should listen to the truth?

LPGA STAR, BARB MUCH, TALKS ABOUT INTERNAL DIALOGUE/SELF CONTROL

In an interview with the *Links Letter,* Barb Mucha talked candidly about what it is like trying to survive on the LPGA Tour. She spoke about how her attitude had been affected at times by what people say, and how she had many times beaten herself up, with her own negative words. When responding to the question, "How do you stop listening to those negative words?," she said, "Negative words or thoughts really aren't the truth about who you really are, but there is one thing that I know is true, God's Word. When I started having negative thoughts, I'd start recalling scriptures to myself, 'I can do all things through Christ who strengthens me,' 'We are more than conquerors through the Lord Jesus,' 'Trust in the Lord with all your ways and lean not on your own understanding.' " In doing this she says that she is better able to free herself from the negative thoughts and focus on the task at hand which is to enjoy the game of golf.

She says that it is almost like God is telling her, "Don't let a golf score take away your joy." She also added, "That must have been what Jesus meant when He said, "The truth will set you free!"

TAKE A MOMENT AND LISTEN TO YOUR INTERNAL DIALOGUE/SELF TALK

If you were to ever take a moment and listen to your internal dialogue right before you give into a temptation, you would notice something very astounding.

Before giving into temptation, you are always listening to a lie!

"You can't quit smoking."
"You can't lose weight."
"Take it easy, you don't need to exercise."
"You can't make 3-foot putts."

That last lie, the 3-foot putt, is the one that I listened to for eight long years. It used to dumbfound me how I could make 100 3-foot putts in a row on the practice green only to miss nearly every one I faced during the actual round. Why was that? I found that it was because once on the course, I started listening to a lie going on inside of my head that said, "Forget it, Tim, you can't make 3-foot putts!" Now I know better because the fact is that I can make 3-foot putts, I've made plenty of them, and I'll make plenty more! Today I'm a different putter, because instead of listening to that lie going on inside of my head, I speak the truth to the lie, and the truth is, "I can make 3-foot putts!"

PUTTING YIP KEY NO. 4—SPEAK THE TRUTH TO LIES AND THE TRUTH IS I CAN MAKE 3-FOOT PUTTS!

What would you rather listen to anyway–a lie or the truth? If you are a person who likes to listen to the truth, consider all the benefits:

1 Corinthians 2:9 "Eye has not seen, nor ear heard, nor have entered into the heart of man, the things which God has prepared for those who love Him."

2:10 "But God has revealed them to us through His Spirit. For the Spirit searches all things, yes, the deep things of God."

2:11 "For what man knows the things of man except the spirit of man which is in him? Even so no one knows the things of God except the Spirit of God."

2:12 "Now we have received, not the spirit of the world, but the Spirit who is from God, that we may know the things that have been freely given to us by God."

2:13 "These things we freely speak, not in words which man's wisdom teaches, but that the Holy Spirit teaches, comparing spiritual things with spiritual."

2:14 "But the natural man does not receive the things of the Spirit of God, for they are foolishness to him; nor can he know them, because they are spiritually discerned."

2:15 "But he who is spiritual judges all things, yet he himself is rightly judged by no one."

2:16 "For who has known the mind of the Lord that he may instruct him?' But we have the mind of Christ."

Now for the important part if you have Jesus Christ living in you, then you have the mind of Christ which 1 Corinthians 2:16 speaks of. Likewise, as a believer you would also have the spirit of God within in you, which 1 Corinthians 2:12 speaks of. Put these two passages together and you come to the realization that the truth is always there, residing within your being.

But how do you know what you are hearing is the truth?

TEST THE SPIRITS!

If you are not sure which spirit you are hearing from test them as 1 John 4:1 says:

1 John 4:1 "Beloved, do not believe every spirit, but test the spirits, whether they are of God."

To test the spirits all you have to do is read the Word of God. The Holy *Bible* is nothing but truth!

A STORY OF SELF-CONTROL

The Bible story of Joseph is about faith and righteousness, but it is also a story about self-control.

In one instance, Joseph had to use self-control in refusing the sexual advances of his master's wife. Several times while her master was away, she attempted to seduce Joseph into committing an unrighteous act. She became so upset at his refusals that she eventually ended up accusing Joseph of rape.

In another instance, Joseph exercised self-control in how he dealt with his brothers after his brothers sold him into a life of slavery. When Joseph eventually became a ruler, he could have had them beheaded, but chose instead to befriend them.

Much like Joseph decided to exercise self-control in both of these situations, on the golf course we have the right to exercise the same kind of self-control. It's up to us, we can decide to walk with peace, kindness, gentleness, joy, love, peace, faith, or we can decide to walk with fear, anxiety, anger, sadness, or depression. The choice is ours to make, and that, in essence, is what self-control is all about!

Now, let's assume you have self-control, then you ought to be able to just say "Yes" or "No" after all of your golf shots, shouldn't you? The subject of the next chapter.

11

Let your "Yes" be "Yes" and your "No" be "No"!

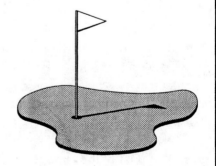

In researching the Bible to find out what we are allowed to say after we hit a golf shot, the only thing that I could find was either to say "Yes," "No," or nothing at all.

Matthew 5:37 "Let your "Yes" be "Yes" and your "No," "No." For whatever is more than these is from the evil one."

CONSIDER HOW SERIOUS THE LORD TAKES SWEARING!

Deuteronomy 5:11 "You shall not take the name of the Lord your God in vain, for the Lord will not hold him guiltless who takes His name in vain."

Proverbs 13:3 "He who guards his mouth preserves his life, but he who opens wide his lips shall have destruction."

Psalm 34:13 "Keep your tongue from evil and your lips from speaking deceit."

James 3:8 "But no man can tame the tongue. It is an unruly evil, full of deadly poison."

James 3:10 "Out of the same mouth proceed blessing and cursing. My brethren, these things ought not to be so."

James 3:11 "Does a spring send forth fresh water and bitter from the same opening?"

Proverbs 18:21 "Death and life are in the power of the tongue, and those who love it will eat its fruit."

Obviously from these scriptures, you can see that we are not to swear, and that includes when we hit a bad golf shot!

YOUR BAD GOLF IS NOT GOD'S FAULT!

When you hit a bad shot, make a bad decision, or make a mental error, it's never God's fault! Nor does your bad golf shot give you an excuse, or permission to swear, especially at God!

It's truly amazing to hear some of the things that come out of people's mouths when they play golf. People who you have never heard swear in their life before, can be found swearing on the golf course. Golf is kind of like hitting your finger with a hammer, you never know what is going to come out of your mouth. Golf, unfortunately at times, has a way of bringing out the worst in people. Why is that?

I think it's because golf, unlike other pursuits in life, has a way of bringing out what's stored within the deepest parts of our hearts. If, for instance, you fill your head all week with things like violence, anger, depression, etc., then out of that abundance you will speak with violence, anger or depression. On the other hand, if you've stored the living word of God in your heart all week then, out of the abundance of your heart will come out righteous words like encouragement, love, etc. Consider what Matthew 12:34 has to say about it:

Matthew 12:34 "Brood of vipers! How can you, being evil, speak good things? For out of the abundance of the heart the mouth speaks."

DON'T CURSE YOURSELF EITHER

We're not to curse ourselves either. If you call yourself an idiot, a dummy, a choker, an uncoordinated ox, a basket case, or any other derogatory term, then that's cussing at yourself, and God doesn't want you doing that either. Consider what He says about it in the following scriptures:

In Matthew 5:35 it says we should not swear "by the earth, for it is His footstool; nor by Jerusalem for it is the city of the great King;"

5:36 "Nor shall you swear by your head, because you cannot make one hair white or black."

Got the point? According to God's holy and non-deniable Word, we are not supposed to cuss, damn or curse at anything, or anybody, including ourselves!

IF YOU SWEAR AT YOURSELF, YOU ARE REALLY SWEARING AT GOD!

If God made us in His likeness, then doesn't it make sense that if we are swearing at ourselves then we are really swearing at God. It would be no different then if you painted a beautiful painting, only to swear at it. In swearing at the painting, aren't you really swearing at the maker of the painting?

When God created us, He didn't make any mistakes, God said in Genesis Chapter 1, that we were created very good!

Genesis 1:31 "Then God saw everything that he had made, and indeed it was very good."

Got the point? God doesn't make any junk, and if He made you, He doesn't want to see or hear you damning yourself or anything else, instead He would much rather hear you say just a simple "yes," "no," or nothing at all!

WHEN YOU HIT A BAD GOLF SHOT, JUST LET YOUR "NO" BE "NO"!

If you feel a need to respond to a bad shot, just say "no!" That doesn't mean "oh no," "blanken no," or any other derogatory word in front of "no," just a simple calm, "no"! Anything more than that is like putting poison into your game.

TAKE THE POISON OUT OF YOUR GAME!

In James 3:8, it says an unruly tongue is full of deadly poison. If you were to drink poison, what would happen? Wouldn't you either get sick or end up dying? Well, that's the same way it is when you let your tongue get out of control on the golf course. Your game is either going to get sick, or it's going to end up dying! Consider what Matthew 12:34 and Proverbs 27:19 have to say about our hearts: Matthew 12:34 "Brood of vipers! How can you being evil, speak good things? For out of the abundance of the heart the mouth speaks." Proverbs 27:19 "As in water face reveals face, so a man's heart reveals the man."

I'm sure it's happened to you before. You start your day off happy and full of cheer, then all of a sudden you start hitting some bad shots, you lose control and you start swearing. Before you know it, you are so frustrated and negative that you make the one comment every golfer seems to make when there is no point of return. You say, "I've never played this badly in my life before," and before you know it, you actually live up to it. You just shot your worst round of golf! Sound familiar? That's what the poison of the tongue can do to your golf game, if you let it!

DON'T PUT A CURSE ON YOUR GAME!

Have you ever stopped to think about what cussing or cursing really means? Consider what the dictionary says.

Cussing - Invoking disaster or calamity upon the object of one's wrath.

Curse - To place a curse on someone would mean to pray or invoke harm or injury to come upon one.

Both of these definitions kind of parallel one another, don't they? It almost makes you think that if we cuss at ourselves, we are also cursing at ourselves.

WHAT PART OF YOUR GAME IS CURSED?

Have you ever felt like a part of your game is cursed? I mean it seemed like whatever you did, the same old problems kept creeping up? As I mentioned earlier, for me it was a problem with 3-foot putts and believe me, if you felt the twitches like I did, you too would think it was a curse!

The curse, though, had one big problem. A witch wasn't cursing me, but I was cursing myself. You see, when I missed a few short putts, I often ended up cursing at myself. I called myself everything, a basket case, a choker, an idiot, a dummy, a loser, etc. These curses eventually led to more missed putts and more curses. It was a miserable cycle that I could never seem to break. That was until I started thinking of cursing and cussing as the same thing. You see, if you think of it as the same thing, the last thing in the world you want to do, is to put a curse on your game. After all, isn't golf tough enough anyway?

PUTTING YIP KEY NO. 5, DON'T CURSE YOURSELF!

Now I'm not sure if you believe in curses or not, but if you are a believer in God's Word, then you have to believe that His words apply in all situations and that includes the situations that we get into on the golf course. Consider the parallel of the following scripture:

Proverbs 15:4 "A wholesome tongue is a tree of life, but perverseness in it breaks the spirit."

Now ask yourself this question. Have you ever used a perverse word on the golf course? Did that perverse word break your spirit? Did it cause you to give up on your game? Did it affect the play of your group? Did your perverse words cause you to lose your focus? Did the golfing atmosphere in your group change? See the parallel.

Now ask yourself this question. Have you ever played a round of golf with a wholesome tongue? The round where you kept control of your tongue for an entire 18 holes? Not hardly once did you use a negative word. Did it help? Did it help the golfing atmosphere of the rest of the group? Was there a wholesome spirit in the air? See the parallel?

Spirits have a lot to do with sports—let your spirits down for just a second and you are sure to suffer. Do you think the NFL thinks spirit is important? You bet they do, how else could you account for them spending thousands of dollars in the hiring of cheerleaders!

GOLFERS DON'T HAVE CHEERLEADERS!

Aside from caddies and the people in our own foursome, golfers, in general, don't have the benefit of cheerleaders, and if there was ever a sport that needed them, golf is it!

Out of all the sports in the world, golf can generally be agreed upon to be the most frustrating. There's just too many things that can go wrong: Errant tee shots, water, wind, trees, out of bounds, bad decisions and, of course, missing those short makeable putts! With all those frustrations going on, it's no wonder that our spirits get down once in a while. Why is that? Why do our spirits get down so quickly? The answer can be found in Galatians:

Galatians 5:17 "For the flesh lusts against the Spirit, and the Spirit against the flesh; and these are contrary to one another, so that you do not do the things that you wish."

You see, your flesh, anger, frustration, depression, etc., wars against your spirit, which is love, joy, peace, faith, long-suffering, kindness, gentleness, and self-control. Now if you are a person controlled by the spirit, then your flesh won't win the war!

BE LED BY THE SPIRIT!

If you are tired of being beat up by the flesh, try walking in the spirit like Galatians 5:16 says:

"I say then: Walk in the Spirit and you shall not fulfill the lust of the flesh."

A person who is led by the spirit can win all battles of the flesh and that includes the battle of frustration!

FRUSTRATION IS A WORK OF THE FLESH

If you were to list some of the main battles of the lust of the flesh, the list would look like the one below, but don't you think you could add frustration to the list?

Mind over Cursing   Mind Over Drinking
Mind Over Sex   Mind Over Smoking
Mind Over Food   Mind Over Drugs
Mind over frustration on the golf course!

Now, just because Corinthians says you have power over Satan, don't you think for a moment that he's just going to go away! Satan has been fighting the war for your mind since the beginning of time and he is still fighting. His biggest weapon, lies! Consider what John 8:44 says about his ability to lie!

John 8:44 "...When he speaks a lie, he speaks from his own resources, for he is a liar and the father of it."

Now with all that lying going on how do we defend ourselves? The answer can be found in Ephesians!

Ephesians 6:11 "Put on the whole armor of God, that you may be able to stand against the wiles of the devil."

12. "For we do not wrestle against flesh and blood, but against principalities, against powers, against the rulers of the darkness of this age, against spiritual host of wickedness in the heavenly places."

13. "Therefore take up the whole armor of God that you may be able to withstand in the evil day, and having done all, to stand."

14. "Stand therefore, having girded your waist with truth, having put on the breastplate of righteousness."

15. "And having shod your feet with the preparation of the gospel of peace."

16. "Above all, taking the shield of faith with which you will be able to quench all the fiery darts of the wicked one."

17. "And take the helmet of salvation, and the sword of the Spirit, which is the word of God."

18. "Praying always with all prayer and supplication in the Spirit, being watchful to this end with all supplication for all the saints."

Now let's take these weapons individually and apply them to

golf, so we can get a better understanding of how to better use them.

Truth - Satan can't fight the truth, because he is a liar and liars hate truth! Satan would want you to believe, for instance, that you were born an alcoholic, a thief, or a bad putter. That's right, I said a bad putter, and if you think you were born a bad putter, that's a lie! You see no one was born a bad putter, it's not hereditary and if you are putting badly, the fact is that you can get better. Consider how some of the following players on the PGA Tour have turned their putting woes around.

Tom Watson - Good Putter to Bad Putter Back to Good Putter
Bernhard Langer - Good Putter to Bad Putter Back to Good Putter
Steve Elkington - Bad Putter to Good Putter
Peter Jacobsen - Bad Putter to Good Putter

The list is endless, but the point is that if you are putting badly, your putting can improve.

Note: Steve Elkington's putting improved dramatically when he won the 1995 PGA Championship. In winning the championship, he out putted second place finisher Colin Montgomery by 14 putts, not bad for a guy who used to consider himself a bad putter.

Breastplate of Righteousness - Satan also can't fight righteousness because everything about him is unrighteous. He would like to do nothing more than get you to commit some kind of unrighteous sin, but if as a Christian you stand tall and fight for righteousness, you won't open the door for Satan to come in.

Example: Not participating in coarse joking on the golf course.

Gospel of Peace - Satan also would like to do nothing more

than to take your peace away from you, but as long as you read and act on what scripture says, there's no way that Satan can do that. No matter what the circumstance!

Example: Someone hits into your group and doesn't apologize!

Shield of Faith - Satan also hates the faithful. If he thinks you are going to be unfaithful, he will hang around until you open up that door. The Bible is full of stories of men of great faith, and in each instance these great men used patience along with faith to win their battles. Satan can't fight against the faithful!

Example: You miss a couple of putts early in the round, and instead of getting depressed and giving up, you use a little faith, with patience, and turn your putting woes around.

Helmet of Salvation - If you are saved, one who has given himself to God, then Satan positionally can't beat you. He can if you let him, but if you don't let him he can't win!

Example: I know I want to have a temper flare, but I'm not going to allow Satan to have this victory! Positionally I'm stronger than him in Christ!

Sword of the Spirit - The sword of the spirit is the Word of God. No matter what Satan does he can't fight against the Word of God. All you have to do is speak the word of God to Satan and it's like sticking a dagger right into the center of his heart, he can't fight it!

Example: You shall not take the name of the Lord thy God in vain.

Prayer - Satan hates it when we pray. Satan also can't fight prayer, no matter what your problem may be. God is in the prayer answering business and he has an answer to all your needs. Prayer is the key to going to war with Satan.

Example: Praying to God to help you control your emotions while playing golf.

LET YOUR "YES" BE "YES"!

When you hit a great golf shot, what should you say? Well if you are using Matthew 5:37 as your guideline, all you should say if you feel an urge to say something positive is, "Yes," or nothing at all!

SAYING SOMETHING MORE THAN YES IS CALLED PRIDING

If you say something more than "Yes," after you hit a great golf shot, saying something like, "I'm the greatest ball striker at this club," that would be considered priding, and God hates pride! Consider what the following scriptures have to say about pride:

Proverbs 16:19 "Better to be of a humble spirit with the lowly, than to divide spoil with the proud."

James 4:6 "…God resists the proud, but gives grace to the humble."

Romans 12:16 "Be of the same mind toward one another. Do not set your mind on high things, but associate with the humble. Do not be wise in your own opinion."

Proverbs 16:18 "Pride goes before destruction, and a haughty spirit before a fall."

Job 40:11 "Look on everyone who is proud and humble him."

Pride was what got Satan thrown out of the heaven, Satan

wanted to be more powerful than God, and because of his pride he was separated from God.

Today pride is readily seen in American sports. Players often seem more interested in themselves and how much money they can make with little or no concern for the fans, or the good will of their teammates or the game. In football, they have this thing called the touchdown dance that receivers do to show everyone what a great feat they performed by scoring a touchdown. As to say "Hey, I'm great, I caught a touchdown." Instead of dancing though, they would be much better served if they would just quietly give the ball to the referee and let their play do the talking.

Players also do a lot of strange things just to stand out, or be noticed. Examples of this would include wearing dark sunglasses during an interview, strange hair cuts, tattoos, exuberant clothes, and jewelry.

These things, too, are examples of priding, especially if they're doing it just to be noticed!

LET YOUR PLAY DO THE TALKING

Have you ever heard a sports star say, "I let my play do the talking"? By design, that's the way sports are supposed to be played. I think that's what God might have had in mind, when he gave David the inspiration to write Proverbs 27:2:

Proverbs 27:2 "Let another man praise you, and not your own mouth; a stranger and not your own lips."

The Post-Shot Routine, Just Say Yes, No, Or Nothing at all 85% Of The Time.

Most of us have a pre-shot routine to hitting a golf ball, but what about a post-shot routine. A routine for dealing with a good, bad, or indifferent shot?

The next time you play golf, try being pro-active, instead of reactive. React to all of your shots with what I call the "Yes/No focus." To do it just simply try to play 18 holes of golf by trying to react to all your golf shots by just saying "yes," "no," or nothing at all. Actually pre-condition your response before you even hit the ball.

For example, if you either verbally or non-verbally tell yourself something like, "No, I didn't plan on hitting that shot out of bounds," this would be an appropriate, pro-active response. An inappropriate, or reactive response would be either verbally or non-verbally, saying something like, "Come on you dummy, you know these greens are slow!" Get the idea?

When you do this experiment, don't even be concerned with your score, instead concern yourself with how many times you successfully stay in a yes/no focus. For example, if you shot 80 and you responded to all of your shots with a simple "yes" or "no" 70 times, that would mean you had a success rate of staying focused 85 percent of the time. Anything above 85 percent is considered good, 95 percent would be considered excellent. I don't know of anyone to date who has actually been successful 100 percent of the time. That would show phenomenal self-control.

Sound easy? Sound positive? It is, and if you try this experiment for 20 straight rounds, before you know it, you won't even have to think about it, just saying "yes," "no," or nothing at all, will become habit forming.

The Post-Shot Routine of Saying "Yes" or "No!"

You've probably heard of the importance of a pre-shot, but what about a post-shot routine, or a routine that you go through after every shot.

In my opinion, a post-shot routine or post-mental routine, is every bit as important as a pre-shot routine.

To use an analogy, what do you say when you leave someone's house—you say "goodbye," right? In other words, you are conditioned to say goodbye. That's what I call a post-shot routine. On the flip side, what do you say when you enter someone's house? You say "hello," right? That's your pre-shot routine, correct?

That's what's so great about having a Yes/No focus. It gives you a pre-conditioned, pro active response to every shot you hit! It, in effect, concludes the shot!

A POST-SHOT ROUTINE WILL HELP YOU CON-CLUDE THE SHOT!

Think about it for a second. How many times have you thought you forgot about a shot, only to find that negative thought still lingering several holes later? It lingers, only because you never forgot it in the first place. You are still mad at the shot!

It's no different than when you have a re-occurring disagreement with someone. You can try to forget it, think you forgot it, but ultimately that same disagreement comes up over and over again, doesn't it? That's because you never concluded the conversation in the first place. It still lingers on!

Bad golf shots are no different than a re-occurring disagreement. They have to be dealt with!

THE PROPER WAY TO CONCLUDE YOUR BAD GOLF SHOT!

What's the proper way to conclude a disagreement with someone? Should you yell at them, tell them they are wrong? Give in to their demands, even though you know you are right? Should you have a rational, yet civil conversation with them? If you chose the third option, you are correct.

Following that line of logic, how then do you conclude a terrible golf shot civilly and rationally? You simply get in the habit of maintaining a pro active yes/no focus!

For instance, let's say you just topped your last brand new Titleist balata golf ball into the water. Being frustrated, what's the proper response if you are using a pro-active yes/no focus?

Just to give you a feel for it, the following responses would be acceptable:

"No, I didn't mean to top it in the water"–said calmly!

"No, I didn't transfer my weight properly"–said calmly!

"No"–said calmly!

"Patience, it will come"–said calmly!

"Okay Tim, let's use a little faith!" –said calmly! "I've been working on my swing, it's going to get better."

Get the idea? You conclude the shot, by being pro-active instead of reactive.

WHY SHOULD I BE PRO-ACTIVE INSTEAD OF REACTIVE?

Two simple reasons: to help you forget, and to help you focus.

Let's face it, how can you expect to realistically forget a shot if you are so emotionally wound up that you always have to react? It's kind of like yelling at someone–once you do it, it's kind of hard to expect things to get back to normal.

Second, how can you expect to stay focused if you react to every little scenario that happens in a round of golf.

Now I'm not saying you need to be a robot when you play golf. No, quite the contrary! Go ahead and play the game with emotions, just keep them in check.

You don't have to be a zombie out there when you play. There is nothing wrong with pumping your fist like Tiger Woods does when he makes a good putt, or getting excited over a good shot. Who knows if you enjoy those good shots a little more, maybe more will come.

Note: Don't underestimate the importance of a yes/no focus. As I mentioned in the beginning of this chapter, in researching the Bible, it's really the only appropriate response!

12

Different Schools of Thought on Golf Psychology

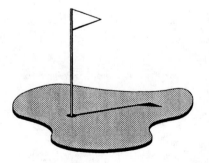

Today there are all kinds of help you can get for your game in the field of Sports Psychology. Collectively, these experts have a variety of techniques aimed at helping their students improve their game. In some cases, these techniques have helped players win championships, while in other instances these techniques have had little or no impact on a player's overall improvement. Why is that? Well, I contend that when it comes to matters of the mind, you can only have limited success in the field of humanistic psychology. That's because as humans we are limited in what we can do, but with God's help all things are possible.

Matthew 19:26 "With men this is impossible, but with God all things are possible."

USE THE BIBLE + GOD AS YOUR PSYCHOLOGIST

The reason you can only have limited success in psychology is due to the way we are made. You see, unlike a machine, the mind of man can't just be fixed! The mind is an enormously complicated machine that not even the smartest of men can figure out!

GOD KNOWS US, EVERY INCH OF US!

Unlike a psychologist, God can assure us that He not only knows us, but knows every inch of us and that includes our minds. After all, wasn't He the one that created the mind? Consider what the following scriptures have to say about creation and psychology:

Jeremiah 1:5 "Before I formed you in the womb I knew you; Before you were born I sanctified you; and I ordained you a prophet to the nations."

Isaiah 9:6 "And His name will be called Wonderful Counselor, Mighty God, Everlasting Father, Prince of Peace."

Genesis 1:26 "Let Us make man in Our image."

Psalm 139:14 "I will praise You, for I am fearfully and wonderfully made."

Psalm 139:15 "My frame was not hidden from you, when I was made in secret, and skillfully wrought in the lowest parts of the earth."

Psalm 139:16 "Your eyes saw my substance, being yet unformed."

In His word, God goes to great detail to explain our emotions, how they are supposed to be used and how they can benefit us all while glorifying God. In other words, the handbook for golf psychology was already there, all we had to do was pick it up, read it, and apply it to our particular sport. That is not to say, however, that there aren't some experts in the field of sports psychology who can help you. There are! As a matter of fact there are plenty of them. What you need to do though, is find somebody that you are comfortable with, just like you would find a golf teacher that you are comfortable with. In the field there are six sports psychologists that have done some terrific work. They are: Dr. David Cook, Carey Mumford, Chuck Hogan, Dr. Deborah Graham, Bob Rotella and Dr. Richard Coop. All of them have worked with over a hundred players on both the PGA, LPGA, Senior and Nike Tours combined, and are available for seminars, lectures, counseling sessions, etc.

DR. DAVID COOK

Dr. David Cook, sports psychologist, President of Mental Advantage, Inc., Fort Worth, Texas, is an evangelical Christian who uses the platform of sports psychology to minister to athletes, coaches, and corporate executives. He is the author of an audio and video tape series entitled *The Psychology of Tournament Golf,* and has spoken at over 80 PGA functions.

During the execution stage of the golf swing, Dr. Cook will have his students use three phrases. They are "see it," "feel it" and "trust it," in that order.

During the "see it" phase, the visualization of the shot takes place: The flight pattern, spin of the ball, the effect of the wind, etc. In the second phase, the "feel it" phase, the kinesthetic feel of the shot is taken into account. In the final stage, the "trust it" stage, the word "trust" is silently said to yourself as you make the swing, by saying this word slowly throughout the swing, it, in effect, keeps other disrupting thoughts from coming in.

CHUCK HOGAN

Chuck Hogan, president of The Learning and Performance Center in Phoenix, Arizona, is the author of the book, *Five Days to Golfing Excellence.* His most notable student is probably Peter Jacobsen.

During the actual shot Chuck stresses the importance of being mentally engaged and physically relaxed.

When you are mentally engaged, you are receiving all of the appropriate instructions from the target. The location definitions surrounding the target, the wind, the elevation, humidity and all the other subtleties are perceived, calculated and processed by keen awareness when you are interested in the target.

In being mentally engaged, you disregard the consequences of the shot and are completely attached to the images you project about the shot at hand. These images have a beginning, middle and end.

The image itself is processed in the mind for only the moments it takes for the swing itself. The quality of the shot is reflected by the images and your engagement with them.

Chuck notes that if you had to develop one of the two performances being mentally engaged or physically relaxed, he said that he would rather you be physically relaxed, although he stresses that the mental and physical are one, not two human experiences.

In his book he uses a self-guided relaxation exercise called autogenetics, which was developed in the 1930's by Dr. Johavan Schultz.

DR. DEBORAH GRAHAM

Dr. Deborah Graham, counseling psychologist, SportPsych, Inc., Boerne, Texas, is a regular writer in the *PGA Journal of Instruction.*

To describe what the zone is, quoting from several unnamed clients that she works with, the scenario reads, "Everything was easy, it was like being in a cocoon where nothing could bother me; I was totally into the round but didn't have to think hard about what I was doing. I didn't feel rushed, rather relaxed and energized, I felt I could do anything, I only had to visualize where I wanted to put the ball and it was there; I was aware of everything, but disturbed by nothing, not even mistakes."

In her article, she uses eight personality traits determined by her study of PGA and Senior PGA Tour players, to distinguish the frequent winners, the champions, from the other players 95 percent of the time. The personality traits where the champions scored differently than the other players are: Focus, abstract thinking, emotional stability, dominance, tough mindedness, confidence, level of arousal and self-sufficiency. Each of these traits being explained in greater detail in her article.

During the shot, Deborah says that playing in the zone usually means that you are so involved in the immediate experience that you allow things to happen. Instead of trying to make them happen, you focus on simple routines and the immediate task at hand, with little thought going into intense analytical thinking about your score, your mechanics, money, etc. You are acting more automatically, letting your body do what it is trained to do.

CAREY MUMFORD

Carey Mumford, clinical psychologist, is the President of ProForm Associates, Crossville, Tennessee, and author of *The Double Connection.*

In Mumford's book, he uses what he calls the clear key. Much like the clear key on a computer which clears the computer screen, he'll have his players use a phrase which in effect clears or quiets the mind.

Here's how it works. A phrase is selected which is long enough to last from the start to the end of the swing. This phrase is repeated three times, or as often as you would like. First, as you are entering the transitional part of the swing, or just before you address the ball. The phrase is then said a second time when you actually address the ball, and finally the phrase is said a third time to trigger the actual swing.

The clear key accommodates the task of neutralizing emotional elements that interfere with the automatic process.

When picking a clear key, it's important that it be passive and have no action command given or applied. It should be rhythmic (capable of reflecting the swing) and fun (makes you smile from your gut), neutral (has no reference to swing, and extended–long enough to start before the swing and last throughout).

Examples of clear keys would be:

"I love palm trees."

"Whatever happened to Absorbing Senior?"
"Sesame Street is the place to meet."

Proverbs 17:22 "A merry heart does good like medicine."

BOB ROTELLA

Bob Rotella, adjunct professor, University of Virginia, is author of *Golf is not a Game of Perfect and Golf is a Game of Confidence.* Bob is also co-author of an audio tape series with Dr. Richard Coop entitled *Mind Power to Better Golf.*

In Bob Rotella's first book, *Golf is not a Game of Perfect,* he writes about several subjects common to all golfers, including: Dreams, trust, confidence, fear, pressure, competition, practice, and more. The book is very straight-forward, simplistic, and full of insight.

In his second book, *Golf is a Game of Confidence,* he writes from more of a perspective view of the Pros themselves. PGA Pros like Brad Faxon, Jay Delsing, Davis Love III, Tim Simpson, Billy Mayfair, Dicky Pride, David Frost, and LPGA Pros Val Skinner, Pat Bradley and others, share their unique insights into how Bob has helped them to focus in all the different areas of their game.

DR. RICHARD COOP

Dr. Richard Coop, sports psychologist, University of North Carolina, is the author of *Mind Over Golf,* how to use your head to lower your score.

In Dr. Coop's book, *Mind Over Golf,* he writes about all the different aspects of the mental game, including the pre-shot routine, concentration, visualization, success, fear, anger, self talk, the demands of golf and more.

Like Bob Rotella's books, his book is pretty straightforward, and doesn't complicate the mental game of golf by going into deep intellectual studies of the mind. It's a very enjoyable read, and should be a must to any golf enthusiast!

A POINT MADE FOR THE RECORDS!

Regardless who you work with, you will have to practice your new mental routine until you get used to it. Just like a new swing change, sometimes new mental routines can take as long as three weeks to get used to. Don't give up though, because as the old axiom goes, "It usually gets worse before it gets better!"

Personally, of all the different methods that I have used, I have found the principles found in Carey Mumford's clear key to be most suitable for me. In using his principle, I use scripture for my phrases during the swing. My favorite one to use is "The peace of God surpasses all understanding." I like this phrase, because when I swing I like to hear the word "peace." At other times, I have been known to use other scriptures that are unique to the emotion that I am going through. For instance if I'm playing golf and I need a little joy, I plug into a scripture with the word "joy" in it. If faith is my problem, I use a verse with "faith" in it; "love," a scripture with "love" in it, etc. I have found that by plugging into the appropriate scriptures I get that little bit of extra reliance I need to swing in an unrestricted way.

Lately, I have found a phrase that seems to help me when I'm putting. The phrase can be found in 1 John 4:18:

1 John 4:18 "There is no fear in love; but perfect love casts out fear; because fear involves torment. But he who fears has not been made perfect in love."

This phrase seems to work well for me, because when I'm putting, I often feel fear, and sometimes torment! The phrase reminds me that yes, I do have an emphatic love for golf, a perfect love if you will. Therefore, if I have a perfect love for the game, that cancels out or casts out any fear, anxiety, or torment.

PUTTING YIP KEY NO.6—FINDING A CLEAR KEY THAT DEALS WITH YOUR EMOTIONS

Between shots I use memory verses to help me focus. The verses help me to maintain a positive frame of mind, and keep negative thoughts from coming in. Thoughts like "I can't putt," "What's wrong with me," etc.

QUOTES ABOUT WHAT PLAYERS ON THE PGA TOUR THINK DURING THE ACTUAL SHOT

Sam Snead: "When I'm approaching the ball, I visualize the shot I want to hit. When I'm taking the club out of the bag, I can still see the shot I want to hit in my mind. When I'm setting up to the ball I can see it, and from there it's a question of going through the movements with my hands, arms, body and what not. To make the shot in my mind's eye. If I'm interrupted when I'm in the process of doing this, I very seldom hit a good shot."

Bobby Jones: "The one thing most likely to assure the most satisfactory progression of the swing is clear visualization in the player's mind of the movement."

Jack Nicklaus: "I never hit a shot, even in practice, without having a very sharp, in focus picture of it in my head. It's like a color movie. First, I see the ball where I want it to finish, nice white setting up high on the nice green grass. Then the scene quickly changes and I see the ball going there: Its path, trajectory and shape, even its behavior on the landing. Then there's sort of a fade out and the next scene shows me making previous images into reality."

THINGS IN COMMON WITH GOLF PSYCHOLOGIST

The movement is automatic, instinctive, reactive.

A word or phrase is said during the swing to keep interfering thoughts away.

The focus is either on visualization or feel or both. (Some teachers use other senses like hearing, smell, and taste.)

Your self-talk is important.

Relaxation techniques and pre-shot routines are used.

Knowing your personality and golfing style is important.

Golf Course Management is important.

Having a basic understanding of your neural muscular system and how it responds to messages sent from the brain is important.

Note: If you would like to have some more information on any of the afore mentioned experts in the field of golf psychology, I have listed them in the index for your convenience.

13

How to Deal with Pressure!

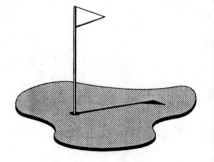

When playing golf competitively, whether it be in a U.S. Open, a club-level event, or an ordinary golf outing, pressure can come in many forms.

We may feel pressure when faced with a 3-foot putt to shoot our best round of golf. Pressure may also be felt when we encounter certain difficult holes, like a long par three surrounded by water with a pin closely tucked to an ensuing hazard.

Pressure can also come from other sources. How about the pressure we put on our own expectations of our game, or the pressure we let others put on us, with their own expectations of us?

Sometimes other factors are involved, especially if you play golf for a living. The pressure of being away from your family and friends, the pressure to put food on the table, the pressure from the media, and the pressure of keeping your job, which so many other aspiring pros would love to have.

Any of these factors, if not properly dealt with, can disrupt a golf game, and possibly ruin it, if you let it!

How then do you deal with these pressures?

Seek to Please God—Not Man!

In studying the issue of pressure relative to golf, it became clear that pressure in golf comes from persuasion, the persuasion of men vs. the persuasion of God.

Galatians 1:10 For do I now persuade men, or God? Or do I seek to please men? For if I still pleased men, I would not be a servant of Christ.

If you were to think about it, everything we do with passion in life is either motivated by our need to satisfy either man or God. If you play golf to satisfy yourself, or others, rather than to please God, then you are really playing golf for man!

Let me explain: Why do wealthy people labor 70 hours a week at a job they hate? Isn't it because they want to buy more things, to accumulate more wealth, to either satisfy their own selfish desires, or to satisfy the desires of others?

Why do people get married for reasons other than love? Isn't it again to satisfy either their own selfish desires or the desires of others?

Finally, why is it that some athletes practice harder than others and sometimes, as a result, end up becoming a professional? Could it be to satisfy either their own lust or the lust of others?

All of these actions, although they may be well intended, actually are contradictory to the way God would want us to live our lives. Consider what 1 Corinthians 10:31 has to say about the subject: Therefore, whether you eat or drink, or whatever you do, do all to the glory of God.

God isn't against hard work, or fame or fortune. What He is against, though, is people who fear man more than God. Consider what some of the following verses have to say about the fear of God:

Psalm 34:9 Oh, fear the Lord, you His saints! There is no want to those who fear Him.

Psalm 111:10 The fear of the Lord is the beginning of wisdom.

Proverbs 3:7 Do not be wise in your own eyes; Fear the Lord and depart from evil.

Proverbs 29:25 The fear of man brings a snare, but whoever trusts in the Lord shall be safe.

2 Timothy 1:7 For God has not given a spirit of fear, but of power and of love and of a sound mind.

Who do you fear when you play golf? Do you fear man or God? What are you more concerned with when you golf–your score or how you please God in shooting your score?

Hopefully, you are starting to understand my point. To take some of the pressure out of the game of golf, you are going to have to learn how to please God, and not man, when you play.

HOW THEN DO YOU PLEASE GOD WHEN YOU ARE PLAYING GOLF?

You please Him with your mouth and with your mind, you please Him with your actions, your attitude and your countenance.

Now if you are a Christian, it is easy to please God when you are playing well, but what about when you are playing poorly?

CAN YOU PLEASE GOD EVEN WHEN YOU ARE PLAYING BADLY?

What do you do when you play poorly? Do you sulk, belly ache, whine, moan, curse, get depressed or angry? Hopefully not!
God would rather see you playing golf in the spirits of love, joy, peace, long-suffering, gentleness, kindness and self-control. Expressed in a formula I think it would look something like this:

Success in Golf = Pleasing God–Not Others, Not Yourself

Think for a moment what an impact that would have on your golfing companions. It might even spur them on to ask you questions like: Why do you never get mad? How do you stay so focused and in control? Where do you go to church, or how can I know this person you keep talking about, Jesus Christ?

PGA Tour Player, Gary Hallberg, Shares A Story

The pressure to live up to expectations can really become intense, especially if you play on the PGA Tour. Consider what happened to Gary Hallberg:

In the January/February 1993 issue of the *Links Letter,* PGA tour player Gary Hallberg shares a story about his life-long struggle of trying to please himself, others and God.

In the article, Gary explains how everything gratifying to him came from his success in golf. In his first year on the PGA Tour, 1980, he played pretty well, finishing in the top 10 six times out of 11 tournaments. This feat still fell short of the expectations put on him by his friends, family, media and himself.

In the next two years, his game got progressively worse and everyone was trying to figure out why he wasn't winning. The fear of letting everyone down made the pressure to win almost unbearable. He started asking himself questions like, "What am I doing out here? What kind of life is this?"

He was playing to please others and himself and he wasn't doing either!

Finally, the pressure let up a little bit in 1983 when he beat out Tom Kite to win the San Diego Open. Winning that tournament, however, was just a small oasis in a huge desert.

The next few years were up and down for Gary. The players he was beating in college were starting to pass him by. Searching for answers he started reading books. He tried everything from philosophy to Zen. None of it helped. As a matter of fact, it was probably more damaging than good, since it was directed at motivating self or self-centeredness.

Finally, in 1990, Gary started to understand his problem when he and his future wife stood up in a church in San Diego and accepted Jesus Christ into their hearts as their Lord and Savior.

In 1990, Gary was to face the biggest battle of his PGA Tour-playing career. Coming into one of the last tournaments of the season, the San Antonio, Texas, Open, Gary needed to make $80,000 to keep from having to go back to the grueling PGA Tour Qualifying School.

Before this tournament started though, he felt a sense of peace. This was different from the anxiety that he had felt in less crucial situations in the past. He didn't have the overwhelming feeling like "Oh no, this is it!"

That week he went to the Bible study on the PGA Tour. The speaker described how Jesus reacted in various situations including the pain and suffering of the crucifixion. He painted a vivid picture of who Jesus was–what He was like–and challenged everyone to live every situation the way Christ would live it. Gary decided to take the challenge and apply it to his golf game in the upcoming tournament.

In the previous 13 weeks he had only made two cuts, so there was no reason why he should expect to suddenly play well. Surprisingly, he found himself on the last hole of the tournament tied for the lead.

After placing his tee shot some 20 feet from the cup on a par three hole, he needed a two putt to tie for the lead, a one putt would win! Unfortunately, he would do neither and three putted to finish second to Mark O'Meara.

The three putt this time meant nothing to him. He had played the whole tournament day-to-day constantly asking himself one question, "How would Christ handle this?" He walked off the green totally elated. It didn't seem to matter whether he came in second, third, or even last. Living to please God–not himself, not others– was what was important.

Today, Gary admits that he wishes he could say that he's living every moment asking the same question, "How would Christ handle this situation?" but admits that at times it's too easy to do things the way Gary Hallberg wants to do them. He realizes it is a process and even today he is still trying to let go and focus on pleasing the Lord.

Like Gary, you, too, can take the pressure off your game by establishing a more personal relationship with Jesus Christ! Golfers like Corey Pavin, Tom Lehman, Gary Hallberg and several others have all talked about the difference in the amount of pressure they felt before they knew Christ and after they knew Christ.

Before you know Christ, life is like living in a bubble. You feel like everyone is looking in and you can't get out. You are the whole and can't find the parts. That adds up to one thing–pressure! When it comes to golf, the less pressure you have, the better off you are.

On the other hand, once you know Christ, or have Him in your life, everything changes. No longer are you in the bubble. You are no longer the whole, but part of the whole, and that adds up to one thing–peace, the opposite of pressure!

Devoid of pressure you can then focus on another part of your game, Golf Course Management. As discussed in Chapter Two, 25 percent of the game can be contributed to golf course management. The rest of your score is determined by how good or bad your technique is, your physical limitations, and how well you mentally manage your game.

Stated again in the 25 percent rule, your golf score is made up of the following four elements:

The game is: 25 percent Mental
              25 percent Technique
              25 percent Physical
              25 percent Course Management

 * a percentage of luck could also be added into this equation.

It then becomes imperative to understand everything there is to know about golf course management, the topic of the next chapter!

14

GOLF COURSE MANAGEMENT

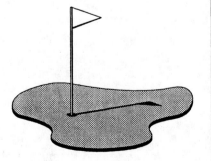

Golf course management begins even before you arrive at the golf course. Here are some of the things that you should consider:

- What clubs should I bring?

- Should I bring an umbrella, towels?

- What clothes should I wear?

- What balls should I bring, gloves?

- What about snacks, fruit?

- Did I stretch out?

- What golf course strategy should I use?

The decisions you make here could very well be the difference between winning a tournament or making the cut.

Assuming you've made those proper decisions, it then becomes important to have an effective pre-game warm-up.

PRE-GAME WARM-UP

Golfers as a group often underestimate the importance of a good pre-game warm-up. A warm-up will not only prepare you for the game, but it will also help protect against some possible injuries.

In just about all other sports, athletes can be found doing exercises to warm-up. It's a scientific fact that our muscles perform better when they are warm. Take football running backs for instance, do you ever see them walk right from the locker rooms onto the playing fields. Not often, right? Well, the same could be said for a golfer. Below are some ideas for a good pre-game warm-up. Try them. Not only will they help you get loose, but they also will protect against unwanted injuries.

AT HOME BEFORE YOU PLAY

Ten to 20 sit ups (crunches)
Twenty to 30 jumping jacks
Ten to 20 reps stretching out legs, arms, back, shoulders
     and wrist.

ON THE PRACTICE TEE

Once you get to the practice tee, stretch again before hitting any shots. Try my golf club stretching exercises.

GOLF CLUB STRETCHING EXERCISES

Reach For The Sky - With the golf club out in front of you, reach for the sky, emphasizing a good stretch. Done properly it will stretch out your sides, arms, shoulders and back.

Side Bends - With the golf club over your head, bend your side to the left and then to the right. This exercise mainly focuses on stretching out your sides and back.

Calf Stretch - With the golf club over your head, slowly bend over and try to place the shaft of the club on the ground. Of all the exercises, this is one of the best because it stretches out the back, calves, thighs, shoulders and arms.

perfectly still and make a 90 degree turn with your shoulders and hips, trying to get the club to face directly behind you. Done properly this exercise will really stretch out the back, sides and shoulders.

Behind The Back - Back And Shoulder Stretch - With the club over your head, reach behind your back and stretch, placing heavy emphasis on stretching out the back, arms, shoulders and sides.

Wrist Stretch - Hold the club directly in front of you and hinge the club to the left and right using your wrist as a lever. Not only is this a good stretching exercise for your wrist, but it helps build strength and flexibility in the forearms, hands and wrist.

Arm And Shoulder Stretch - Hold the club on both ends and turn the club back and forth until it reaches a horizontal position. Start with an SW, if you work with this exercise consistently you should eventually be able to get a 3, 4, or 5 iron to a perfect horizontal position.

* When doing these exercises try to do five to 10 repetitions of each, paying particular awareness to muscles in the back, shoulders and wrist. These are usually the first muscles to go when you get injured in golf.

ONCE STRETCHED, PLAY 18 HOLES ON THE PRACTICE TEE!

If you are getting ready to play, the practice tee is there for two reasons. First, to help you get loose and secondly, to help you find out what your tendencies will be once you get on the golf course. That's why I think it's very important to play a practice 18 holes, before you actually play.

To play a practice 18, simply visualize each hole and play it, just as if you were on the actual course. Once on the course you can then draw from your experience on the practice tee and play to those tendencies.

PLAY TO YOUR TENDENCIES

In playing to your tendencies, all you are really doing is guessing what each club will do. Consider some of these examples to clarify what I mean by guessing. "Will it barely hook, or hook a lot?" "I'm not hitting my long irons very far, so I guess I'll try a 5 wood." "When I try to really kill it, I lose it a little right, so I'm going to aim at the left side of the fairway and let it drift back to the center."

Note: As a rule of thumb, always play to your tendencies, unless you can't!

Sometimes as golfers, our games don't always go that well. At times it might seem as though you couldn't even hit the broad side of a barn. Ever hear that one before? It's on days like these that playing to our tendencies won't help. I mean, what good could come from a ball that plops right out in front of you, or flies straight right, out of bounds? Not much, right? That's when you need to use a swing key, any key, just some technique that will get you around the course, and in the clubhouse.

PUT THOSE BAD GAMES BEHIND YOU

If you have one bad round, don't worry about it, put it behind you. If you have two bad rounds, go to the practice tee and work it out. If you have three bad rounds, then maybe you need a little help, it may be time to see a PGA Professional.

All too often golfers change their whole game around just because they have a bad round. Immediately they start pouring into the pages of golf instructional magazines, searching for the secret swing key that's going to get them on track, only to never find it. Oh, they may think they find it one day, but the next day it's a whole new key. So on and on they go searching and searching, only to never find what they need.

Let me ask you a question. When your favorite sports team loses, do you think it would be a good idea to dwell on the loss, to fire the coaches, to revamp the entire offensive and defensive schemes? Depending on who your team is, that answer could be a "yes," or "no," but statistically speaking, if your team has one bad game, there's nothing to fret, two bad games, and I still wouldn't worry, it's only when you see prolonged periods of bad play that there's a reason for concern.

The point: Just because you play one bad round, don't change your whole game around. Two bad rounds, get some practice in. Three bad rounds, and you better go see someone who knows the golf swing inside and out, a PGA Teaching Professional.

THE FIRST TEE JITTERS

Do you ever get the first tee jitters? If you do, try what I call the play shot! The play shot is a club or a shot that you play when you need to make sure that you put a shot into play.

I play a shot that I call the three-quarter driver. Rather than taking a full swing with a driver and ripping away at it, I take a three quarter swing, and hit a little fade.

To play it, I simply open my stance a little bit, choke up about an inch on the club, swing slightly outside in and hit a low fade. Since it's a smaller movement and I don't have to swing at it very hard, it's the perfect shot for me to hit any time I feel the pressure to put a ball in play.

Your play shot might be a 5 wood or a 3 wood. Whatever it is, find a club or shot that you are very comfortable with, something you know you can put into play, nearly every time.

CALCULATE YOUR CURVE

Golf is really a guessing game. Aren't you really guessing where your ball is going to go every time you hit it? You bet you are and that's why it's so important that you know how to calculate your curve. To calculate it just guess, that's right, guess! Guess how far left or right you leave your driver, your 7 iron, your pitching wedge, etc. Give me a golfer who knows how to guess, and I'll give you a golfer who knows how to play!

One of the best guessers to ever play the game has to be Lee Trevino. While his technique may be a little unorthodox, Lee, in reality, figured out a shot years ago that gives him a tremendous advantage over his competition. Why? Because he knew where it was going even when he missed it!

The shot that Lee Trevino plays is a low fade that starts straight down the left side of the fairway, or in the case of a green, the left side of the pin and then moves back to the right. It never hooks!

Think about that for a second. If you hit a shot that you absolutely knew wasn't going to hook, then aren't you really taking the left side of the golf course out of play? You bet you are, and that's why I like to say a good guesser always knows how to play!

THE TEEING GROUND

In selecting an area to tee off from, always tee it up on the same side that the trouble is on. When executing the shot, work the ball away from the trouble and then work it back towards it. Visually and mentally that's the easiest way to play the shot, and if you miss it, your chances of ending up in trouble will be far less likely.

THE APPROACH SHOT

Where and how you are going to attack the hole on the approach shot should depend mostly on the following factors:
- Your proximity to the hole
- Your ability to play the shot
- The difficulty around the green
- The slope of the green
- The firmness of the green
- Your angle
- Your position in the tournament

PROXIMITY TO THE HOLE

How close you are to the hole can be good, bad or indifferent. John Daly, who is the longest hitter on the PGA Tour, hits it so far that he often hits it past all the trouble, often leaving himself with only a pitching wedge to the green. This can be a tremendous advantage on some holes, but on others it can be a huge disadvantage.

Depending on what borders the green, big drives can often leave a player in even more trouble. Problems like long grass, elevated greens, and uneven lies are typical when a player's ball goes too far.

The tip here: Be aware of where the trouble is before you rear back and rip it!

YOUR ABILITY TO HIT THE SHOT

If you find yourself with the option of whether to go for it or to play safe, try what I call the 70 percent rule. For instance, let's say you are faced with a 230-yard 3 wood into a green guarded by water left. Should you go for it or lay up? As a rule of thumb just ask yourself this question: Could I pull this shot off seven out of 10 times without getting into trouble? If you can answer "yes," go for it; if "no," lay up!

DIFFICULTY AROUND THE GREEN

When deciding what area of the green to shoot at, decide what area of the green you would rather miss. For instance, if you were hitting into a green that was flat in the front and sloped downward behind, then the best option would be to choose a club that would leave you on the front side of the green.

THE FIRMNESS OF THE GREEN

Most players never take the time to think about the firmness of the greens. Due to the nature of the weather, greens can often change from day to day and often from hour to hour. If the wind picks up, for instance, the greens could go from being soft in the morning to firm in the afternoon. Players who don't calculate this factor often end up bouncing over.

THE ANGLE TO THE GREEN

The angle that you choose to the green can have a huge effect on how close your approach shot gets. Factors like hazards between you and the hole, slopes and the depth of the green can all come into play based on the angle that you decide to choose to come in from.

The tip here: Choose the right angle to come in from!

YOUR POSITION IN THE TOURNAMENT

At times, depending on your position in the tournament, it might be worth risking it, especially if it means winning or losing the tournament.

One thing to remember though in risking it all: You must remember that you cannot walk on water. If I remember correctly, there was only one person that could ever walk on water and his name was Jesus Christ!

THE PITCH OR CHIP SHOT

You should never take a double bogey from just off the green! Golfers all too often play the wrong shots around the greens and end up with a double bogey or worse.

When playing chip or pitch shots around the green, always remember two rules: (1) Get the ball rolling as soon as possible; and (2) Always try to hit it low before you hit it high.

Get It Rolling First - It's always easier to judge the distance of a chip or pitch shot if you can roll it to the hole rather than fly it. In rolling the ball, you have a shorter swing and are more able to control factors like accuracy, distance, and speed.

Always Try To Hit It Low - Always try to hit a shot low before you hit it high! There's just too many things that can go wrong with a high shot: Sculling it, fluffing under it, not hitting it the right distance, and miscalculating the wind, are common mistakes.

WHEN TO HIT PITCH SHOTS HIGH

The only time you should hit a high pitch shot is when the pin is tucked, the grass between you and the green is high, and the slope of the green drops off behind the pin. Even then sometimes the safest shot to play is a one to two hopper onto the green.

The tip here: Hit it low, get it on the green rolling as soon as possible and only go high as your last resort. If you can hold to these cardinal rules, then double bogeys from just off the green will become a thing of the past.

ON THE GREEN, THE PUTT!

A lot of factors go into reading a putt and they should all be considered:
Slope often matches terrain - When you walk up to a green, take note of the hills and slopes surrounding it. Most of the time the green will slope away from the highest slope.

Also look for the nearest water hazard or mountain, the green will usually slope towards it.

READ THE GRAIN

If the grass is slick or shiny, the ball will have a tendency to roll faster. If the grass is dark or rough looking, that means the grain is against you and the ball will have a tendency to roll slower. The grain usually follows the sun.

READ THE CROWNS BY THE HOLE

Don't forget to look for little crowns by the hole. A little crown snuggled up next to the hole can shoot your golf ball off line faster than the tallest mountain in the vista.

THE PHILOSOPHY OF THE PUTT!

• When you are close to the hole, focus on accuracy. When you are far away from the hole, focus on distance. From five feet and in, you usually don't want to aim outside the hole.

• On breaking putts, focus on how hard you want to hit the putt through the apex of the break.

• On uphill putts, be more aggressive and on downhill putts be careful.

• On quick sidehill putts, bring the ball in from the side of the hole instead of the front of the cup. It will eliminate some of the lip-outs and give you a bigger circumference of the hole to work with.

• Keep your grip pressure constant, light is best!

• Watch how your competitor's ball breaks.

• Watch how your ball breaks before and past the hole.

• Aim it and stroke it, the rest is the green's fault!

• You never miss a putt, you just misread them!

• Don't get careless when putting, pitching, or chipping, these shots add up quicker than a drive off a tee or an iron shot into a green.

• When you have a prolonged period of putting badly, you may be trying too hard. What you may need to do is let it happen, instead of trying to make it happen.

Instead of forcing yourself to make putts, focus on keeping a quiet mind. From the moment you take your putter out of your bag until you pick your ball up out of the hole, try to keep a quiet mind, or think about nothing!

• Try not to get overly excited or distressed after each putt. Don't allow your emotions to yo-yo up and down throughout the course of 18 holes. If you do, it will only wear you down, and the result will only be more missed putts.

PUTTING YIP KEY NO. 7—THINK ABOUT NOTHING

As I have mentioned throughout this book, for eight years I had a horrible case of the putting yips. Oh, I might find a technique that works for two or three days, and sometimes up to three weeks, but invariably I always went back to yipping those short makeable putts. Why was that? One of the biggest problems I found was that I was putting too much priority on the putt. My priorities were way out of whack! Making that par or birdie putt literally meant everything to me. If I made it I felt great, but not if I missed it. When I missed an easy one, such as a putt from three feet and in, immediately it felt like someone took my last breath right out from under me. Emotionally I felt dead.

Finally, one day as I was playing a beautiful golf course in Florida with a member, it hit me, "I was trying too hard." After hitting just about every fairway and green for 12 consecutive holes, emotionally I just couldn't take the letdown of missing another short makeable putt. So I gave up! I decided right then and there, that for the remainder of the 18 holes, I would try to think about nothing, from the moment I took my putter out of my bag until I removed my ball from the hole, I was to think about nothing.

Initially, I 3-putted the first two holes. It was uncomfortable thinking about nothing. Soon after though, I got comfortable with it. As a matter of fact, it got so comfortable that I decided that I would commit to thinking about nothing for a full three weeks.

It's been over two years since I tried that little experiment and you know what? Thinking about nothing seems to be the key! Kind of funny, isn't it? To think for all the hundreds of techniques, putters, and gadgets that I tried over the last eight years, the whole key was to think about nothing!

Today I actually enjoy putting more than I ever have, and it's all because of my determination to think about nothing.

WHY IS THINKING ABOUT NOTHING THE KEY?

Let me explain: As a golfer, I have been fortunate enough to play approximately 1,000 rounds of golf in my life. That's 18,000 holes, or approximately 36,000 putts. That is, if I averaged a two putt on every hole, throw in some practice putts, and I guarantee you that I have hit at least 50,000 putts in my life.

With all that practice wouldn't you think that I would have developed some pretty good instincts for putting? Unfortunately, I didn't and it was because for eight arduous years I was too busy thinking about how to putt, rather than letting it happen or thinking about nothing.

Remember some of the putting yip keys that I mentioned throughout this book, keys like: Faith in a technique, patience, our internal dialogue, cursing at ourselves, and the clear key.

All these keys are great, but I still had to find a way to put them into practice.

The answer was finally found when I came up with the following routine that I use when I play golf.

The routine is to say nothing, to do nothing, and to think about nothing. Now I understand what putting unconscious means!

WHAT DO I MEAN BY NOTHING?

To explain what I mean by nothing, let me reiterate. Don't think about the line of the putt, or the speed of the putt, don't think about whether it's for par or birdie. Don't even think about being positive or making it, just think about nothing. Also, don't do anything like jump up and down when you miss a putt, or don't say anything when you either make it or miss it. Don't say something like, "I hit that putt too hard."

Let me explain why that's so important. What happens when you say something like, "I hit that putt too hard?" Isn't your next shot usually short? And what happens when you say something like, "I couldn't make a putt if it was to save my life."? Don't you struggle to make your putts the rest of the day?

I believe our priorities and attitude have everything to do with our behavior. Everyone that putts badly, putts badly not because of a lack of desire, but perhaps too much desire. By placing too much emphasis on one putt, you are more likely to choke under the extra pressure.

Often times a choke, or pressure is caused by outside or inside influences (either other people or ourselves). For instance, if you hit a great iron shot to two feet, it would be easy to think something like, "If I make this it will be a birdie," or "If I miss this I'll look foolish in front of the guys." If you're honest with yourself these types of thoughts will come into your mind from time to time. The key then is to push those thoughts out of the mind when they enter. You do that by saying to yourself, "I'm supposed to be thinking about nothing."

You see, nothing can replace God. Not money, not fame, and yes, even your putting stroke or your golf score.

Some players think they can solve their putting problems by thinking positively. This theory works when they are making putts, but not when they start missing them.

When they miss their shots, their positive thinking lets them down. Therefore, their entire round of golf is emotionally up and down like a yo-yo.

This theory doesn't work because the golf ball doesn't care how positive you are. If you continually blame yourself for mental mistakes, it won't be long before you start to miss more shots.

That's why a say nothing, do nothing, think nothing putting routine is so effective. It won't let you down as much when you miss a putt because you weren't thinking about anything in the first place. Now that's what I call a pro-active approach to putting, not a re-active approach!

Try it the next time you play. What do you have to lose? If you are like most of us, you haven't found a putting technique that lasts longer than three weeks. If you have, congratulations. You are one of the lucky ones, so stick with what works for you. But if you haven't found something that works, why not try what I suggest?

Notes: When you practice, think about good solid putting fundamentals 25 percent of the time and then think about nothing the other 75 percent of the time.

When you play, think about nothing 100 percent of the time (some of you might want to use a clear key as described on page 121 to help you think about nothing).

BERNHARD LANGER AND HIS BATTLE WITH PUTTING

Bernhard Langer is arguably one of the best ball strikers ever. However, no one understands the putting yips as well as him.

His problem with the yips dates back to 1975 when he first started playing on the European tour. Back then, the only thing that kept him going was the knowledge that he was a very good ball striker, and the belief that if he could improve his putting, he could become a great player.

His poor putting continued in 1978. In fact, in one match play tournament, he four-putted from three feet. He was "yipping" it so badly, he would actually hit the ball twice. His opponents would not give him a one-foot putt because they knew he might miss it.

Finally, he broke through in 1979 winning the World Championship. However, every tournament was not a success for him. Putting, was at times, still his biggest enemy.

You may recall in 1985 the first year he won the Masters, he putted conventional on long putts and cross handed on short ones. That worked for quite a while, but eventually the dreaded yips would return.

That's when Bernhard had to rely on his faith: having the knowledge that God wanted him to persevere so he could become a better putter.

He did, and that's when the Bernhard Langer grip was born. He places his right hand around the lower part of his left forearm. He said, "by changing my mechanics, the mental side relaxed and I became more relaxed and positive. Realizing, that I could not do it by myself and giving it over to God, also made all the difference."

You may recall seeing him use that grip when he won the Masters for the second time in 1993. Although he didn't hole every putt in that tournament, his faith, patience, and reliance on God was enough to last all the way to the very last hole and very last putt!

What about you? Does your putting stroke need a little more peace or freedom from self reliance? Could you use a little more patience when you putt? Could you possibly be placing too much importance on making your putt! Should God be more of your priority, and not your putts?

If that sounds like you, then maybe you need to turn your putting over to God. If God will help you use peace, and patience in your personal life, then don't you think he would want you to use it in your recreational life? You bet he would, and he would love to show you how!

HOW TO JUDGE THE WIND!

If the tops of the trees are moving, that's 10 m.p.h. of wind. If the clothes you are wearing rustle, that's about 20 m.p.h. of wind. If the trees are blowing over, that's about 30 m.p.h. of wind. Each 10 miles of wind should be equal to about one club length in distance.

WHICH CLUB TO USE, WHAT'S THE DISTANCE?

There are a lot of ways to figure out how far from the hole you are and which club to use. A lot of courses have markers, marking 200,

150- and 100-yards. Some courses even put yardage markers on sprinkler heads to give you a better idea of how far you are to the hole. Additionally, some courses even use the red, white, blue flag system, all in an effort to let golfers know exactly how far it is to the pin.

Once you have your yardages figured out, then choosing the right club becomes the essential ingredient to a good shot. It therefore becomes extremely important that you know just how far you hit each club. As a general rule ask yourself this question, "What club could you hit to the back of the green, if I hit it perfectly solid?" Grab one more club than that one and swing within tempo.

IF YOU DON'T KNOW, MARK IT!

If you are unfamiliar with how far you hit a club, mark it! Simply, put a piece of masking tape under the grip of all your clubs marking the distance each club goes. You can even be more systematic by marking the distance for a quarter swing, half swing, three quarter, and full swing.

IF THE PIN IS BACK TAKE LESS CLUB, FORWARD, TAKE MORE

One way to be relatively sure that you hit a green is to take less club if the pin is back and hit it hard, or take more club if the pin is up front and hit it normal. That way you will always leave the ball on the side of the pin that has the most green to work with. Everyone should have a distance where they feel they can take dead aim at a pin. A pro might take dead aim from 170 yards, where a higher handicap golfer should only take dead aim from 130 yards or so.

If The Pin Is Left, Aim Right—If It's Right, Aim Left

Another sure way to increase your chance of hitting the green is to aim for the side of the pin that has the most room. For instance, if the pin is on the right side of the green, try to place your ball left of the pin. How far left or right of the pin you choose should depend on how straight you are hitting the ball that particular day.

What To Do To Calm The Nerves

Being nervous when we play golf is common to everyone. Even the best players in the world get nervous. The question then is, how can we relax our nerves enough so we can play our best?

Physically there are several things we can do. They are: Breathe, don't breathe, relax, yawn, laugh, whistle, take vitamins and minerals, quit the caffeine, and control our emotions!

Breathe—To relax our nerves by breathing, just take a couple of deep breaths and exhale slowly.

Don't Breathe—To calm the mind and to keep the body still, Jack Nicklaus has been known to hold his breath when he putts.

Relax—To relax focus on relaxing all of your muscles. Start by relaxing the muscles in the neck, forehead and jaw and work down to your upper extremities, your chest, shoulders and arms and then finally work down to your lower extremities, namely, your legs, knees, ankles and feet. This exercise is commonly used by a lot of psychologists.

Yawn—Lee Trevino often uses this technique as a way to relieve his tension when he's in competition.

Laugh—Lee Trevino obviously uses this technique. It is built into his character.

Whistle—Fuzzy Zoeller, Lee Trevino, and World Series of Golf champion, Mark McCumber all use the sport of whistling.

TAKE VITAMINS AND MINERALS

The best form of preventative medicine can be found in supplements. Adding nutrients like Vitamins C and B have a positive effect on the central nervous system. Caffeine has a negative effect!

As a golfer I have always felt that my nerves were too jumpy, but I never figured it out until one day a friend of mine told me that his putting got much better after he quit the caffeine. Amazingly it makes a noticeable difference!

PUTTING YIP KEY NO. 8—GET OFF THE CAFFEINE AND TAKE VITAMINS AND MINERALS

Control Our Emotions - Mentally there is only one thing we can do to control our nerves and that's to control our emotions. Let any emotion get out of control, like anger, and you're setting yourself up to be a basket of nerves.

There you have it. Golf course management all rolled into a nutshell. Obviously there's more, and I would need more pages than this book is designed to fully cover this subject. With that in mind I would like to make a suggestion. Read two books: Tom Watson's *Strategic Golf* and Chi Chi Rodriguez's *101 Super Shots*. I consider these two books to be a "must read" to any golf enthusiast, and to anyone who wants to know more about golf course management. Both of these books are listed in the index.

CONCLUSION, CHRISTIAN GOLF PSYCHOLOGY

Golf is a wonderful game! To the naked eye it looks incredibly easy, but in reality it's incredibly complicated. Just when you think you have it all figured out, the game humbly reminds you of your frail human qualities.

Golf is also a game that requires a disciplined practice schedule, all the while balancing the other priorities in life, like God first, family, and then career.

Golf is also a game that requires complete emotional control. Emotions like love, joy, peace, long-suffering, kindness, gentleness, faith and self-control can all be used to the benefit or the detriment of our game.

Invariably when we play golf, we are going to either hit good shots or bad shots. How we react to these shots is of the utmost concern to our emotional stability. Taking too much pride in a shot by saying something more than a simple "Yes" can actually harm our game, while saying something more than a simple "No" can have an equally negative effect.

Should we have complete control over our emotions, it still does not guarantee that we are going to hit a good shot! Several other areas of our game can still fail us, including our technique, physical limitations, and our golf course management skills.

Even if all of those areas are in order, without a precise pre-shot routine during the actual shot, we're still destined for failure. Interfering thoughts like fear or worry, if not properly dealt with, can easily disrupt the flow of a good golf shot.

Throw all that together and it makes you want to forget about everything—just think about nothing when you play golf. The only problem with that is when you try to think of nothing you always end up thinking about something anyway, usually when you least need it! To alleviate that process, several sports psychologists have come up with different techniques which will enable a player to focus better during the actual moment of truth, impact!

Even if you succeed in all these different areas, a player still needs to learn how to deal with pressure, either pressure that someone else puts on him or her, or pressure that one puts on himself or herself. Should you be able to accomplish all that for only one shot, then you have played the game of golf, which we must remember is only just a game!

15
INDEX

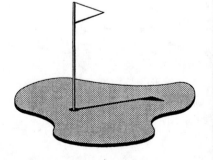

101 Supershots
Chi Chi Rodriguez with John Andrisani
Harper and Row Publishers, New York
10 East 53rd st.
New York, NY 10022

Tom Watson's *Strategic Golf* with Nick Seitz
Publisher, NYT Special services, Inc.
A New York Times Co.
5520 Park Ave., Box 395
Trumbell, CT 06611-0395
(Pocket books a subdivision of Simon and Schuster, Inc.)

Dr. David Cook
President, Sports Psychologist
Mental Advantage, Inc.
5055 Sunscape Lane South
Fort Worth, Texas 76123
(817) 294-8295

Carey Mumford
Sports Psychologist
202 North Main St., Suite 110
Crossville, Tennessee 38555
(615) 788-6758

Dr. Deborah Graham
Counseling Psychologist
SportPsych Inc.
P.O. Box 1976
Boerne, Texas 78006
(210) 537-5044

Chuck Hogan, Sports Psychologist
Sports Learning and Performance

3636 East Baseline Rd.
Phoenix, Arizona 85040
(602) 437-1490

Bob Rotella, Sports Psychologist
GTS Inc. Golf Training Systems
3400 Corporate Way, Suite G
Deluth, GA 30136
(800) 772-3813

Dr. Richard Coop
Sports Psychologist, University of North Carolina
101 Peabody Hall
Chapel Hill, North Carolina 27599 CB 3500
(919) 966-5266

Books and Magazines worth getting for the Christian Athlete

The Links Letter
4216 Evergreen Ln, Suite 134
Annandale, Virginia 22003
The Links Letter grew out of the PGA Tour Bible Study Group in 1980. Published bi-monthly, the Links Letter seeks to link pro and amateur golfers in an informal, worldwide family in Christ, encouraging golfers to use their golf for the glory of God.

Cross Training Publishing
Christian Golf Psychology
P.O. Box 1541
Grand Island, Nebraska 68802
(308) 384-5762
Cross Training Publishing has published over 50 books ministering to the needs of the Christian athlete.

Fellowship of Christian Athletes, *Sharing the VICTORY* Magazine
8701 Leeds Road
Kansas City, Missouri 64129
(800) 289-0909
A movement to present to athletes and coaches, and to all whom they influence, the challenge and adventure of receiving Jesus Christ as Savior and Lord.

Four Skills To Better Golf
974 South Shore Drive
Lake Waukomis, Missouri 64151-1444
Written by PGA Professional Tim Underwood and author of *Christian Golf Psychology,* a book which is quickly gaining popularity as one of the easiest, do-it-yourself, style of golf teaching books. It simplifies golf by breaking it into four basic common denominators.

CHRISTIAN GOLF PSYCHOLOGY TIP SHEET

The intention of this book is not to confuse or overload you with a bunch of new mental swing thoughts. Instead, its purpose is to simplify the mental game of golf. Basically this whole book could be summed up in two areas: What we think and do before, between, or after the shot, and what we think or do during the shot.

Dealing With Thoughts Before The Shot

1. Before the shot, learn to control your emotions: Love, joy, peace, long-suffering, faith, kindness, goodness, gentleness and self-control.

2. Use the post-shot routine by saying, "Yes," "No," or nothing at all 85% of the time.

3. Remember golf is just a game, not a priority. God, on the other hand, is a priority and should be your first priority in life.

4. Self-control is the ability to make a decision and do the right thing. If you are having a problem with self-control, the answer can be found through Jesus Christ.

5. Pressure comes from either the pressure you put on yourself, or the pressure we let others put on us. The only one we really need to please when we play golf is God, not others, and not ourselves.

6. Being in tune with God does not necessarily equate to good golf, remember the 25 percent rule?

7. Use the fruits of the spirit when you play golf.

8. Instead of playing golf with anger, use joy.

• If you are under stress, use peace.

• If you are playing badly, use long suffering.

• If you are playing with someone who is unkind, use goodness and kindness. Have a plan to deal with unkind people. Treat them like you would want to be treated and cheer each other on.

• If you get a bad break like rolling up against a tree, remember that you love the game, not hate it!

• If anger is boiling up inside of you, counteract it with the spirit of gentleness.

• Have faith in your abilities, not confidence, but faith!

• Don't listen to your internal lies, speak the truth to the lies.

• Use memory verses, proverbs, or prayer to help you keep your focus on what's important when you play golf, serving God, not yourself, not others!

Dealing With Thoughts During The Shot

1. During the shot just say a phrase. Pick a scripture that puts you in a positive frame of mind.

2. Stay in the present, don't let thoughts about the past or future enter in.

Scripture/Golf Memory Verses

Memorize these verses so you can better understand and deal with the different emotions that you experience in a round of golf.

Love - (Love is not a feeling, it's a commitment!)

Deuteronomy 6:5 "You shall love the Lord your God with all your heart, with all your soul, and with all your strength."

Psalm 119:97 "Oh, how I love your law! It is my meditation all the day."

Proverbs 10:12 "Hatred stirs up strife, but love covers all sin."

Song of Solomon 2:4 "He brought me to the banqueting house, and his banner over me was love."

Song of Solomon 8:6 "Set me as a seal upon your heart, as a seal upon your arm, for love is as strong as death."

Matthew 5:44 "But I say to you, love your enemies, bless those who curse you, do good to those who hate you and pray for those who spitefully use you and persecute you."

John 3:16 "For God so loved the world that He gave His only begotten Son, that whosoever believes in Him should not perish but have everlasting life."

John 15:12 "This is My commandment, that you love one another as I have loved you."

John 15:13 "Greater love has no one than this, than to lay down one's life for his friends."

1 Corinthians 13:4 "Love suffers long and is kind; love does not envy; love does not parade itself, is not puffed up."

13:5 "Does not behave rudely, does not seek its own, is not provoked, thinks no evil."

13:6 "Does not rejoice in iniquity, but rejoices in the truth."

13:7 "Bears all things, believes all things, hopes all things, endures all things."

13:8 "Love never fails."

1 John 4:11 "Beloved, if God so loved us, we also ought to love one another."

1 Peter 4:8 "And above all things have fervent love for one another, for 'love will cover a multitude of sins.'"

1 John 4:18 "There is no fear in love; but perfect love casts out fear, because fear involves torment. But he who fears has not been made perfect in love."

1 John 4:19 "We love Him because He first loved us."

1 John 4:21 "And this commandment we have from Him: That he who loves God must love his brother also."

1 John 5:3 "For this is the love of God, that we keep His commandments. And His commandments are not burdensome."

1 John 2:15 "Do not love the world or the things in the world. If anyone loves the world, the love of the Father is not in him."

1 John 4:8 "He who does not love does not know God, for God is love."

1 John 4:10 "In this love, not that we loved God, but that He loved us and sent His Son to be the propitiation for our sins."

Psalm 33:5 "He loves righteousness and justice, the earth is full of the goodness of the Lord."

Proverbs 17:17 "A friend loves at all times, and a brother is born for adversity."

John 12:25 "He who loves his life will lose it, and he who hates his life in this world will keep it for eternal life."

John 14:21 "He who has My commandments and keeps them, it is he who loves Me. And he who loves Me will be loved by My Father, and I will love him and manifest Myself to him."

Ephesians 3:19 "To know the love of Christ which passes knowledge; that you may be filled with all the fullness of God."

Romans 5:5 "Now hope does not disappoint, because the love of God has been poured out in our hearts by the Holy Spirit who was given to us."

Joy (God's joy is continuous, happiness is only circumstantial)

Philippians 4:4 "Rejoice in the Lord always, again I will say, rejoice!"

Isaiah 12:3 "Therefore with joy you will draw water from the wells of salvation."

Psalm 16:11 "You will show me the path of life, in Your presence is fullness of joy."

Psalm 30:5 "Weeping may endure for a night, but joy comes in the morning."

Psalm 43:4 "Then will I go to the altar of God, to God my exceeding joy, and on the harp I will praise you, O God, my God."

Isaiah 65:14 "Behold, My servants shall sing for joy of heart."

Jeremiah 15:16 "Your words were found, and I ate them, and Your word was to me the joy and rejoicing of my heart; for I am called by Your name."

Matthew 13:20 "But he who received the seed on stony places, this is he who hears the word and immediately receives it with joy."

John 15:11 "These things I have spoken to you that My joy may remain in you, and that your joy may be full."

John 17:13 "But now I come to you, and these things I speak in the world, that they may have My joy fulfilled in themselves."

1 Thessalonians 2:19 "For what is our hope, or joy, or crown of rejoicing? Is it not even you in the presence of our Lord Jesus Christ at His coming?"

1 Thessalonians 2:20 "For you are our glory and joy."

Hebrew 12:2 "Looking unto Jesus, the author and finisher of our faith, who for the joy that was set before Him endured the cross, despising the shame, and has sat down at the right hand of the throne of God."

James 1:2 "My brethren, count it all joy when you fall into various trials."

3 John 1:4 "I have no greater joy than to hear that my children walk in truth."

Psalm 100:1 "Make a joyful shout to the Lord, all you lands!"

Peace

Numbers 6:26 "The Lord lift up His countenance upon you, and give you peace."

Psalm 4:8 "I will both lie down in peace, and sleep; for You alone, O Lord, make me dwell in safety."

Psalm 34:14 "Depart from evil, and do good; seek peace and pursue it."

Isaiah 9:6 "And His name will be called Wonderful, Counselor, Mighty God, Everlasting Father, Prince of Peace."

Isaiah 26:3 "You will keep him in perfect peace, whose mind is stayed on You, because he trusts in You."

John 14:27 "Peace I leave with you, My peace I give to you; not as the world gives do I give to you. Let not your heart be troubled, neither let it be afraid."

John 16:33 "These things I have spoken to you, that in Me you may have peace. In the world you will have tribulation; but be of good cheer, I have overcome the world."

Romans 5:1 "Therefore, having been justified by faith, we have peace with God through our Lord Jesus Christ."

Ephesians 2:14 "For He Himself is our peace, who has made both one, and has broken down the middle wall of separation."

Philippians 4:7 "And the peace of God, which surpasses all understanding, will guard your hearts and minds through Christ Jesus."

Colossians 1:20 "And by Him to reconcile all things to Himself, by Him, whether things on earth or things in heaven, having made peace through the blood of His cross."

Colossians 3:15 "And let the peace of God rule in your hearts, to which also you were called in one body, and be thankful."

2 Peter 1:2 "Grace and peace be multiplied to you in the knowledge of God and of Jesus our Lord."

Matthew 5:9 "Blessed are the peacemakers, for they shall be called sons of God."

Long-Suffering And Patience

Psalm 86:15 "But you, O Lord, are a God full of compassion, and gracious, longsuffering and abundant in mercy and truth."

1 Thessalonians 1:3 "Remembering without ceasing your work of faith, labor of love, and patience of hope in our Lord Jesus Christ in the sight of our God and Father."

1 Timothy 1:16 "However, for this reason I obtained mercy, that in me first Jesus Christ might show all longsuffering, as a pattern to those who are going to believe on Him for everlasting life."

Romans 15:5 "Now may the God of patience and comfort grant you to be like-minded toward one another, according to Christ Jesus."

James 1:4 "But let patience have its perfect work, that you may be perfect and complete, lacking nothing."

Kindness \ Goodness \ Righteousness

Isaiah 54:10 "For the mountains shall depart and the hills be removed, but My kindness shall not depart from you."

Romans 12:10 "Be kindly affectionate to one another with brotherly love, in honor giving preference to one another."

Ephesians 4:32 "And be kind to one another, tenderhearted, forgiving one another, even as God in Christ forgave you."

2 Peter 1:7 "To godliness brotherly kindness, and to brotherly kindness love."

Psalm 23:6 "Surely goodness and mercy shall follow me all the days of my life; and I will dwell in the house of the Lord Forever."

Psalm 52:1 "Why do you boast in evil, O mighty man? The goodness of God endures continually."

1 Timothy 6:18 "Let them do good, that they may be rich in good works, ready to give, willing to share."

Romans 2:4 "Or do you despise the riches of His goodness,

forbearance, and longsuffering, not knowing that the goodness of God leads you to repentance?"

1 Peter 3:17 "For it is better, if it is the will of God, to suffer for doing good than for doing evil."

Colossians 1:10 "That you may walk worthy of the Lord, fully pleasing Him, being fruitful in every good work and increasing in the knowledge of God."

Romans 12:21 "Do not be overcome by evil, but overcome evil with good."

Proverbs 17:22 "A merry heart does good, like medicine. But a broken spirit dries the bones."

Proverbs 12:28 "In the way of righteousness is life, and in its pathway there is no death."

Deuteronomy 6:18 "And you shall do what is right and good in the sight of the Lord, that it may be well with you, and that you may go in and possess the good land of which the Lord swore to your fathers."

Romans 5:7 "For scarcely for a righteous man will one die; yet perhaps for a good man someone would even dare to die."

Gentleness / Meekness / Humility

Philippians 4:5 "Let your gentleness be known to all men. The Lord is at hand."

Matthew 11:29 "Take My yoke upon you and learn from Me, for I am gentle and lowly in heart, and you will find rest for your souls."

Matthew 5:5 "Blessed are the meek, for they shall inherit the earth."

Luke 1:78 "Through the tender mercy of our God, With which the Dayspring from on high has visited us."

Colossians 3:12 "Therefore, as the elect of God, holy and beloved, put on tender mercies, kindness, humility, meekness, longsuffering."

Job 40:11 "Disperse the rage of your wrath; look on every one who is proud and humble him."

Isaiah 57:15 "I dwell in the high and holy place, with him who has a contrite and humble spirit, to revive the spirit of the humble, and to revive the heart of the contrite ones."

Zephaniah 3:12 "I will leave in your midst a meek and humble people, and they shall trust in the name of the Lord."

1 Peter 5:5 "...Yes, all of you be submissive to one another, and be clothed with humility, for 'God resists the proud, but gives grace to the humble.'"

1 Peter 5:6 "Therefore humble yourselves under the mighty hand of God, that He may exalt you in due time."

Proverbs 27:2 "Let another man praise you, and not your own mouth; a stranger, and not your own lips."

Faith

Habakkuk 2:4 "Behold the proud, His soul is not upright in him; But the just shall live by his faith."

Matthew 6:30 "Now if God so clothes the grass of the field, which today is, and tomorrow is thrown into the oven, will He not much more clothe you, O you of little faith?"

Matthew 17:20 "Because of your unbelief; for assuredly, I say to you, if you have faith as a mustard seed, you will say to this mountain, 'Move from here to there,' and it will move; and nothing will be impossible for you."

Mark 4:40 "But He said to them, 'Why are you so fearful? How is it that you have no faith?'"

Romans 1:17 "For in it the righteousness of God is revealed from faith to faith; as it is written, 'The just shall live by faith.' "

Romans 3:22 "Even the righteousness of God through faith in Jesus Christ to all and on all who believe. For there is no difference."

Romans 3:28 "Therefore we conclude that a man is justified by faith apart from the deeds of the law."

Romans 10:17 "So then faith comes by hearing, and hearing by the word of God."

2 Corinthians 5:7 "For we walk by faith, not by sight."

Ephesians 2:8 "For by grace you have been saved through faith, and that not of yourselves; it is the gift of God."

Ephesians 4:5 "One Lord, one faith, one baptism."

2 Timothy 4:7 "I have fought the good fight, I have finished the race, I have kept the faith."

Hebrews 11:6 "But without faith it is impossible to please Him, for he who comes to God must believe that He is, and that He is a rewarder of those who diligently seek Him."

James 2:18 "But someone will say, 'You have faith, and I have works.' Show me your faith without your works, and I will show you my faith by my works."

Deuteronomy 7:9 "Therefore know that the Lord your God, He is God, the faithful God who keeps covenant and mercy for a thousand generations with those who love Him and keep His commandments."

Luke 16:10 "He who is faithful in what is least is faithful also in much; and he who is unjust in what is least is unjust also in much."

Hebrews 10:23 "Let us hold fast the confession of our hope without wavering, for He who promised is faithful."

1 John 1:9 "If we confess our sins, He is faithful and just to forgive us our sins and cleanse us from all unrighteousness."

Psalm 119:90 "Your faithfulness endures to all generations; You established the earth and it abides."

2 Timothy 2:13 "If we are faithless, He remains faithful; He cannot deny Himself."

Self-Control

2 Timothy 3:3 "Unloving, unforgiving, slanderers, without self-control, brutal, despisers of good."

2 Peter 1:6 "To knowledge self-control, to self-control perseverance, to perseverance, godliness."

The story of Job.
The story of Joseph.
The story of Jesus.
The story of the Bible.